WORK APPRECIATION FOR YOUTH

The WAY to Work

An Independent Living/Aftercare Program for High-Risk Youth

A 15-Year Longitudinal Study

AMY J.L. BAKER   DAVID OLSON   CAROLYN MINCER

Foreword By Nan Dale, President/CEO, The Children's Village

CWLA PRESS
WASHINGTON, DC

CWLA Press is an imprint of the Child Welfare League of America. The Child Welfare League of America (CWLA), the nation's oldest and largest membership-based child welfare organization, is committed to engaging all Americans in promoting the well-being of children and protecting every child from harm.

CHILD WELFARE LEAGUE OF AMERICA, INC.
440 First Street, NW, Third Floor, Washington, DC 20001-2085
E-mail: books@cwla.org

CURRENT PRINTING (last digit)
10 9 8 7 6 5 4 3 2 1

Cover design by James Melvin
Text design by Michelle Peña, Capitol Publishing Corporation

Printed in the United States of America

ISBN # 0-87868-804-8

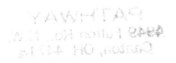

Contents

Tables

Figures

Acknowledgments

There are many people who played an important role in the development and implementation of this 15-year study of the Work Appreciation for Youth (WAY) Scholarship program. First, we would like to thank the youth who participated in both the program and the comparison group. These young men shared their thoughts and feelings with project staff, completed data collection forms, and generally made themselves available over several years. Their courage and perseverance in facing their many life challenges is nothing short of awe-inspiring.

The success of the WAY Scholarship program is directly attributable to the commitment of the program staff to the values WAY sought to impart, and especially to their love and devotion year in and year out to the young people they served. Simply put, they were crazy about the kids and they let them know it even when the kids were at their most difficult. The program has had the usual staff turnover challenges but those currently in place deserve special mention as they helped collect data and interpret the program to the authors. We especially wish to thank Candace Rashada, Director of WAY Scholarship and the following WAY counselors: Saul Lichtine, Carl Morton, Nicholas Stewart, Daniel Stiel, Robyn Tolliver, and Joanne Washington. And finally, we would like to acknowledge Nan Dale, CEO and President of The Children's Village (CV). The WAY program was her dream. Through her untiring commitment to the boys at CV, she made that dream a reality.

Foreword

Nan Dale, President/CEO
The Children's Village

It would be difficult to imagine a more at-risk population than adolescents in residential treatment centers (RTCs), the child welfare system's most restrictive level of care. Since the advent of the Child Welfare Reform Act two decades ago, only youth with severe levels of behavioral or emotional problems, layered on top of the issues of abuse and neglect, have been approved for the costly intervention of residential treatment. For New York City, that represents only 4% of the roughly 40,000 young people in the foster care system. Generally, these are highly troubled adolescents with a history of failed foster home placements, psychiatric hospitalizations, or early run-ins with the juvenile justice system. They are, as one professional in child welfare calls them, the "frequent fliers" of the system. There is credible evidence that these adolescents are among those at greatest risk of adult criminality, educational failure, and continuation of a cycle of dependency. Their prognosis is not good. No one would buy stock in their futures.

It is for this population that the WAY program, the subject of this report, was originally invented. WAY stands for Work Appreciation for Youth, but it is much more than an employment program. It encompasses what much of the field refers to as "youth development," what school officials call "drop-out prevention," and what the child welfare community now refers to as "independent living skills." It is all these things; but most importantly, for youth leaving the foster care system, it is also a long-term "aftercare" program. Though WAY was first designed for this very high-risk population described, it has since been adapted to other populations of disadvantaged youth. WAY provides the support and guidance that *all* young people need to make the transition from adolescence to adulthood—support that is critical for youth transitioning from residential treatment back to their homes or into independent living arrangements and for youth living in highly at-risk family situations.

The WAY study is the first and only longitudinal study of what happens to adolescents leaving residential treatment who have been provided long-term follow-up services focused on school, work, and personal development. The results speak for themselves: low attrition rates, remarkable school success, strong employment experience, and overall impressive evidence that the young people in WAY have been set on a solid path toward self-sufficiency. Based on these results, we believe public policies that affect adolescents who are discharged from the child welfare system need to be modified to allow for interventions such as WAY, which has been possible up to this point only because of the support of private donors. Further, we believe that the overall configuration of youth employment programs, school drop-out prevention, and independent living programs need to be modified to support the kind of comprehensive, developmental, and long-term approach that has made WAY successful where other interventions have failed.

The adolescents we serve at The Children's Village (CV) RTC have, all too frequently, been reared in grotesque poverty and in communities, and sometimes in families, that resemble war zones. Nonetheless, they are also, in many ways, just ordinary adolescents. They march to the rules of peer pressure no less strictly than the hordes of suburban teens that mimic each other with alarming precision. But the norms of these teens' environment have required conformity to standards of behavior that robbed them of their education, their health, and their identity. Much of what we do at CV involves inspiring youth to make their own choices to shape their own future—and, to embrace their humanity against a tide of peer pressure and their injured childhood. We watch them do so everyday—against all odds. They become dissenters and revisionists, reclaiming a healthy identity as they nudge themselves, their families, and their communities toward change. It is not always easy to be there with and for them. It is not easy to help them relinquish their despair and their rage. To remove their armor and dive into the treacherous waters of dissent takes great courage. Our work with these youth is about providing the guidance and calming the undertow for them. It is about giving them the strength and the skills to make responsible choices and to "fall out" from the crowd and the negative expectations that surround them.

Among the skills most needed are those associated with becoming self-sufficient adults: a decent education, the attitudes and ethics needed for successful employment, and a belief in oneself and the possibility of controlling one's own future. The WAY program was initiated to do just that. WAY defines the preparation of young people for the world of work broadly.

WAY starts early and lasts longer than typical youth development programs. It is not a quick fix, but rather a program that works gradually by providing consistent, ongoing support. WAY takes an individualized, developmental, long-term approach to youth employment and includes academic, attitudinal, and employability skills along with the belief that each young person needs to feel that at least one person has a strong stake and interest in his success—and will be there for him.

In recent years, there has been a growing consensus among researchers and practitioners that, in order to be successful, youth employment programs must be comprehensive, long-term, and multisystemic. WAY is built on all those principles and adds further evidence that programs that approach workforce preparation in ways that are too modest, too brief, or that lack continuity over time do not work. For youth coming out of the foster care system—a foster home, residential treatment, or group home—the challenges are especially serious. We have a special need and an opportunity to get it right for a group of youth for whom society has so far gotten it wrong.

Public policy is inching toward recognizing this need; but, even though support for preparing youth for the transition from residential care is growing, it is still far short of what is needed. When WAY was first developed in 1984, the words "independent living" were not yet in the legislative lexicon. In 1987, Title IV-E was passed by the federal government, allocating funding to the states for independent living skill development, job training, and preparation for employment. Each state developed its own specific regulations in accordance with the federal mandates. In most states, the programs were confined to teaching specific skills in a workshop format (e.g., how to fill out a job application, how to write a resume, how to search for a job) to youngsters still in foster care. In most instances, the work—and the funds—stopped once the young person was discharged from foster care. This has been true even though there was an expectation for "supervision to age 21." To the extent this supervision rule has been carried out at all, most agencies simply tell residents at the time of discharge that they can call the agency for help, and an individual is assigned to try to telephone the young person a couple of times a year. Very little actual aftercare service is delivered.

Federal funding for independent living from 1987 to 1999 (which was based on a 1984 population estimate) was static, regardless of the number of youth eligible to receive the services. In 1999 the funds were increased, but they are still not adequate. It should be noted that aspects of WAY are now financed through this funding stream but that the aspect of WAY that is most important, the *aftercare* component called WAY Scholarship, is not eligible for funding. It is the WAY Scholarship program that is the subject of this book.

Several specific steps need to be taken to reshape existing policies, if we are to fulfill the intentions of preparing youth to be able to be self-sufficient as adults. These are discussed more fully in the report that follows. Our recommendations primarily focus on the need for trained, professional mentors to be an ever-present force in the lives of each adolescent leaving residential treatment—for a long time—no matter where he is going. Our recommendations stress that the "mentor" must be a paid professional.

This recommendation seems contrary to the current, volunteer mentoring movement and the positive findings associated with well-run mentoring programs. Indeed, CV supports such initiatives and operates a volunteer mentoring program for some of our residents through a federal Department of Justice grant. Nonetheless, for the population in question, we do not believe volunteer mentors are the same thing, or the right thing, as the paid professional mentor or "counselor" on whom the WAY program relies. The reason we make such a strong statement is because of what we know about the staggering weight of the baggage that most adolescents carry with them to residential treatment. If, in the course of their stay, they are able to unpack a lot of it and learn to cope, they nonetheless still carry a heavy load. These youth are suspended between a painful past and a shaky future.

When they leave residential treatment, if we have done our job well, they are far stronger and positively motivated to succeed. Yet, old hurts and reflexive behaviors have a way of resurfacing when life's pressures intrude. These youth need constancy and predictability to sustain their gains and to help them overcome the hardest times. They need an adult who will pursue them when they waiver, show up at the school house door, or go out to the street corner to guide them away from old haunts and old habits. They need someone who knows the ins and outs of school placements, housing options, symptoms of drug use, and college financial aid packages. They need someone who will not go away, even when told they are not wanted or needed. All of this is simply too much to ask of a volunteer.

In the 15 years that we have been operating the WAY program, we have learned a great deal, and we have made mistakes. In 1994, CV received a grant from the U.S. Department of Labor/Employment Training Administration to replicate WAY in three states in four different community-based settings. These projects were our first "WAY

Partnerships," carried out over four years with local organizations that responded to our Request for Proposal for replication of the WAY program. These community-based organizations targeted out-of-school youth and relied on an adaptation of WAY concepts. Overall, our outcomes were mixed—some quite good, some not so good. In the process, we acquired a far better idea about what kind of strategies we need to employ in future replication work.

Building on our Department of Labor experience, we are now in the process of replicating WAY in a variety of sites around the country—both community-based and with youth leaving foster care. The project that is most developed at this time involves the grafting of the entire WAY program onto a housing complex in east New York for formerly homeless families. Our partner in this project is the (HELP) organization that operates Genesis Homes. Early results are extremely promising. In its third year, HELP assumed full responsibility for the program, with decreasing technical assistance from CV's WAY Replication Unit.

It is because of the variety of sites and organizations that we have now worked with in replicating WAY that we also feel equipped to make some judgments about the process of program development itself. First, forums for comparing program ideas and conclusions are needed. Agencies struggling to find new and different ways to reach young people who are, at best, on the fringes of society need a place to compare notes and to learn from one another. The work of the National Youth Employment Coalition in identifying PEPNet awardees (Promising and Effective Practices Network) and hosting forums has been a welcome initiative. However, there is little cross-fertilization among and between programs. What happens in the world of "youth employment" rarely is heard in the "foster care system," any more than those contending with employment in the "juvenile justice" field hear about the issues other systems are grappling with under different program or funding categories.

Findings, even proven outcomes, from one field do not get incorporated—or even known—by related fields. The youth, however, permeate the various systems regularly, leaving a trail of unfinished business and disconnected attempts to help them. Cross-program mechanisms need to be implemented.

Finally, there needs to be greater recognition of a simple fact: it takes time for results to appear—for programs and for young people. The development of the WAY program has broken all the rules. From the beginning, the program has benefited from the extraordinary support of private donors who were deeply committed to the program *over a long period of time.* They understood that it would take many, many years of funding to allow for program modifications and research to yield results worth the attention of others. Most private funders want "innovative" programs and lose interest in maintaining funding after a few years, regardless of program success or growing pains. The private donors who have supported WAY's development scrutinized our growth while, at the same time, giving us room to make mistakes. Most importantly, they insisted on quality research throughout—and paid for it.

For young people, too, change comes slowly and grudgingly. True "results" are not really meaningful until the program participants become adults. In a world that expects quick fixes and one-word answers to complex questions, long-term solutions are not especially welcome. But, new and different ways to articulate our expectations and measure our successes are necessary. What if, for example, we could find a way to link services for adolescents to how program participants fared as adults? Assume, for a moment, that one could reliably predict the adult unemployment or incarceration rates for youth who are abused as children, or for those who have been arrested more than "x" times before their 16th birthday, or who have been in the foster care system more than "x" years, and so on. Then, suppose that funding for a particular youth program was tied to its success, defined by the number of youth in the program that defied that destiny—e.g., 10% less youth unemployed between the ages of 21 and 30 than predicted yields 10% more funding for the youth program to add new participants. Such an approach—establishing bottom line outcomes based on the long-term success of program participants in the labor market—would channel public resources to the right programs and help bring credibility to a field that is too often viewed by the public as wasteful and without merit.

The book that follows provides the detailed data that allow for a fair and honest assessment of the WAY program but, for those of us who have had the privilege of knowing the youth behind those numbers, no research report can reveal the story we want told. The researchers who have compiled this material have worked hard to give the numbers a face and a name by including quotes and case vignettes. For me, it will never be enough. I am among those who have gotten to know many of these youth, and I marvel at their humanity and the strength and tenacity they have found in overcoming amazing odds. WAY has perhaps been a catalyst in helping them to unleash in themselves a furious desire to oppose themselves to fate. Because, for them, it is not just that it has not been a level playing field, it is that the field has been so onerously tilted against them and mine fields have been so randomly planted that any success at all would be cause for celebration. That they have excelled is an expression of hope.

■ ■

Commentary

Gary Walker, President
Public/Private Ventures

Twenty-five years ago there was great enthusiasm among social policy and program designers, and public and philanthropic funders, for initiatives aimed at high-risk youth. Today there is not. What happened?

It is easy to pin this decline in enthusiasm and funding on a broad shift to the right in American politics. Certainly that shift took place; and certainly that shift has influenced decisions regarding social initiatives and their funding levels. It is folly to think that the world of programming for high-risk youth has its own life apart from broader social and political trends.

But this reading of the history of policy and funding for high-risk youth is, I think, much oversimplified, and thus not entirely accurate. And by trading in the more complicated story of these past several decades for the simple comfort of moral superiority—*we* care and *they* do not—we *add* obstacles to the already difficult challenge of making progress, both in terms of effective policies and programs for high-risk youth.

The dominant themes of high-risk youth policies and programming of the past several decades are two-fold:

 ◆ First, that almost every time a credible long-term evaluation was done, it concluded that the policy or program did not make much if any difference in youths' lives. This is the blunt part of the story, and no amount of anecdotes or critique of research methodology can overcome it.

 ◆ Second, that once the evidence was in—be it neutral, negative, or even somewhat positive as it occasionally was—decisionmakers and funders most often moved on to other initiatives. This is the more nuanced part of the story, for it has less to do with good or bad intentions, or with level of "caring," than it does with the expectations and structure of policymaking and funding institutions. For expectations were that policymaking was like oil drilling: you kept digging holes until you hit a gusher. It was fast work; if no gusher came, there were always other kinds of riches to search for.

The structure of policymaking and funding institutions, in both the philanthropic and public sectors, fit that expectation perfectly: they are most often able to stick with a particular effort for three to five years; and then their own dynamics, be they dominated by public elections or shifting internal interests, cause them to move on.

In this manner, the weight of poor results accumulated. It is no surprise that enthusiasm declined, even among many of those who genuinely care about high-risk youth. Poor results and shifting politics have been a devastating duo.

During the 1980s, there began a steady drumbeat of criticism from many advocates, practitioners, and researchers that the programs evaluated were insufficient to begin with: they were not comprehensive, holistic, or long-term; thus, their poor results were to be expected. Both theory and common sense were used to support this critique.

During the 1990s, a further twist was added: that most youth-serving organizations were underfunded and institutionally weak, and that too often poor results simply reflected weak implementation.

Both critiques seem right to me. But their implications pose very serious practical challenges: What in practice do comprehensive, holistic, and long-term *mean?* And how in practice *do* you build strong institutions? These are tough enough issues in an environment committed to and structured for their solution—but we are in an era whose commitment is shaped by a shift in politics not inclined toward social policy experimentation, and by a steady diet of poor results. We are also in an environment whose policy and funding institutions are not well structured to tackle those issues.

Thus we have entered the 21st century in the toughest sort of policy gridlock around high-risk youth issues: our public policy commitment is weak; our institutions, both funding and operational, do not seem well structured for serious changes in intervention strategy; and, even if both the above could be magically changed, we have few if any concrete, proven examples of *what to do.*

There is a chicken-and-egg aspect to this gridlock: how can you prove what to do if you have weak policy commitment and inadequate institutional structures; likewise, how can you build policy commitment and convince institutions to change if you cannot persuade policy and institutional leaders you know what to do—and that it works?

That is why this study of The Children's Village (CV's) WAY initiative is so important. It describes a program that has well-defined operational components that take the mystery out of "comprehensive," "holistic," and "long term;" that is aimed at a group of youth who meet anyone's definition of high risk; that is run by a highly respected organization; and that *gets positive results*. The WAY program gets these good results by building on the one solidly established piece of knowledge we have about effective interventions for high-risk youth: that it takes strong relationships with adults—mentors—to see a youth through the challenges and transitions that are part of making personal progress.

The WAY initiative is not an easy program to run, as this report makes clear. Nor is it easy to replicate, as Nan Dale's comments indicate. But it is also not a magic show: with appropriate policy and funding support, it can be implemented by solid organizations with caring, competent staff.

Changing lives that for whatever reason have gotten off to a bad start is very hard work. It should not be such a surprise to us that the first several decades of effort showed just how hard it is. The greatest loss from those decades has been the loss of hope that lives can in fact be changed through social interventions.

The results of the WAY initiative should go some way to restoring that hope. We live in a very practical, bottom-line-oriented society—it just may be that empiricism is sometimes the necessary foundation for inspiration. If that is, as I suspect, the case regarding social policy for high-risk youth, then those with funds and voices have several clear tasks in the coming decade:

◆ Make the WAY results known. Repetition, not innovation, is what builds awareness. Results, not rhetoric, persuade.

◆ Find other examples of solid organizations with a track record of serving high-risk youth and carry out credible evaluations. Friends of the Children in Oregon, Hope for the Children in Illinois, Baker House in Massachusetts—these examples come to mind right away, and I am sure there are others. We need to rebuild a base of evidence that inspires hope.

◆ Mine these examples for their implications for policy and funding decisions. It is time to move beyond the guidepost language of "comprehensive," "holistic," and "long-term"—and say exactly what we mean by those terms vis-a-vis practice and cost. That will make good policy and funding decisions—and effective interventions like WAY—more likely.

Besides producing positive results, WAY also reminds us of another hopeful fact: that high-risk children do not exist in impossibly large numbers. Sometimes in the rush to characterize the flaws in American society, we—both liberals and conservatives—exaggerate their consequences. In fact most youth, even from poor conditions, become good parents, good neighbors, and economically self-sufficient. High-risk youth exist in modest numbers; those numbers are not overwhelming, if we have a clear sense of what to do and how to do it.

We owe a great deal to Nan Dale and CV's staff for creating WAY, for seeing it through, and for being far-sighted enough to want, from the very beginning, to document with hard evidence what they were doing and accomplishing. They have used a credible comparison group; they have tracked youth to the age of 21 and beyond—almost unheard of in the world of youth programs; and they have used both self-report and public data in arriving at their findings. In short, they have been responsible in their evaluation approach and have risked arriving at conclusions they might not like. They have also, in their attempts to analyze the association between counselor characteristics and outcome, taken an initial step toward unpacking the "black box" of why an intervention works or does not work.

CV has laid a solid foundation for the rest of us to build on, whether we are policymakers, funders, practitioners, or evaluators.

Executive Summary

A half million young people in the United States are living in foster care. Most of these children and adolescents reside in foster homes. However, there is a subset of the foster care population that is considered so emotionally or behaviorally disturbed that the youth are unable to live in a foster home and are referred to the foster care system's most restrictive level of care, residential treatment centers (RTCs). In New York City, only 4% of the foster care population is in RTCs or other group settings. The Children's Village (CV) RTC, the largest in the system, serves some 400 boys[1] each year. Nearly all have had multiple, prior out-of-home placements and hospitalizations, and all have severe emotional or behavioral problems. Most are poor, from ethnic minority backgrounds, and from some of the most impoverished neighborhoods of the greater New York Metropolitan area. These children are at extreme risk for negative life outcomes including educational failure, unemployment, and criminality.

The odds against them are formidable and the chances of their becoming self-sufficient and productive adults are not in their favor. Prospective studies have documented the many hardships that youth exiting the foster care system face, including homelessness, lack of access to health and mental health services, and difficulties completing their education and finding full-time employment (e.g., Westat 1991). Moreover, retrospective data provide some insight into the long-term outcomes. For example, according to Roman and Wolfe (1997), almost 40% of homeless individuals are former foster care youth. A recent survey of inmates found that 14% of prisoners had lived in a foster home or agency at some point during their lives (Harlow 1998).

The Work Appreciation for Youth (WAY) Scholarship program was developed at CV in 1984 to interrupt this grim trajectory for those leaving the RTC, in an effort to set these youth on a path toward a hopeful future. The program was designed for youth transi-

---

1. CV serves a co-educational population in all of its community-based programs and some of its residential services but only boys in the RTC.

tioning from residential treatment back to their families and communities, to less restrictive settings, or to independent living. As its name implies, WAY Scholarship is a youth employment program. But it is also a general youth development program, a drop-out prevention program, an independent living program, an aftercare program, and a mentoring program. The goals of the WAY Scholarship program are to teach youth work ethics, provide them with opportunities to learn how to work, and encourage them to stay in school and to save and plan for their future.

Created over 15 years ago, WAY Scholarship incorporates many of the elements now considered by policymakers and researchers to be essential for successful youth programs (Kazis & Kopp 1997; Walker 1997). For example, researchers at Manpower Demonstration Research Corporation (MDRC 1983, p. 16) concluded, "The two most important elements of a stable labor market experience are a sound basic education and a combination of work habits, attitudes, and skills." It is just this combination that is at the heart of the WAY program. Moreover, policymakers agree that successful youth programs must be comprehensive and provide youth with a stable, long-term relationship with a caring adult. Individualized and intensive counseling and mentoring over a period of years is the mechanism through which all WAY Scholarship services are delivered.

PROGRAM DESCRIPTION

The full WAY program instituted at CV has five levels, tailored and sequenced for youth while they live in the RTC environment and after they are discharged from care. Levels 1 to 4 are referred to as "WAY Works" and comprise all of the components of WAY that take place on the RTC campus and the surrounding community. WAY Works has the primary goal of teaching work ethics.

♦   All youth residing on CV campus participate in Level 1 of WAY, performing nonpaid chores within their cottage.

♦   Level 2 youth perform small jobs in their cottage or neighborhood for token payment.

♦   Level 3 youth work in low-paid jobs (considerably below minimum wage) at one of CV's campus employment sites (e.g., computer lab, greenhouse).

- ◆ Level 4 youth work at paid jobs off campus (e.g., local hospitals, stores, day care centers).

- ◆ Level 5, WAY Scholarship, is the highest level of the program for youth who are about to be discharged from care. Enrollment is limited because the program has been funded through private dollars in the absence of public funding for aftercare services. WAY Scholarship is the aftercare component of WAY. It is dubbed "Scholarship" not because youth in the program have excelled academically, but rather to set a tone for the higher expectations the program wants to communicate to its participants. WAY Scholarship is a five-year program that provides aftercare services to its participants from the time the youth enters the program (before being discharged from care) until the youth has been in the program five years.

The five core elements of WAY Scholarship are:

1. *educational advocacy and tutoring* to facilitate school success;

2. *work experiences and work ethics training* to enable participants to build work histories and a sense of themselves as workers;

3. *group activities and workshops* to promote a positive peer culture and help youth develop life skills;

4. *financial incentives* to help youth plan, save, and believe in their futures; and

5. long-term, individualized *counseling and mentoring* to help WAY participants meet challenges and solve problems.

It is the counseling and mentoring component that serves as the connection between the youth and all WAY Scholarship services. Once enrolled in the WAY Scholarship program, each scholar is assigned a paid, professional WAY counselor with whom he can develop a relationship that forms the core of the WAY experience. The WAY counselor is the essential ingredient in the delivery of the service, ensuring that youths receive advocacy, information, encouragement, work ethics education, counseling, and other services as needed to succeed in school and on the job. The counselor is to provide personal and intensive emotional support and practical guidance at every step of the way in the youth's young adulthood. Counselors are to be coaches, cheerleaders, surrogate parents, advocates, teachers, and friends. Most important, they aim to "hang in" there with each youth no matter how far off track he strays. In fact, when a youth is most troubled is exactly the time when the counselor is most needed, conveying the very important message to the youth that the counselor will never give up on him. In contrast with the current movement for volunteer mentors (Mech et al. 1995), the WAY program hires and trains paid professional mentors. It was believed that hiring professional staff would increase the likelihood that mentors would be able to make a long-term commitment to the youth.

The five core elements are based on the following assumptions:

♦ Employability and the acquisition of basic education skills are linked.

♦ The development of work ethics (e.g., self-discipline, cooperation, responsibility) and a work history at a young age will supply youth with skills and attitudes that can help them obtain and maintain employment at an older age.

♦ Program components must be developmentally appropriate, and work experiences must be carefully sequenced.

♦ A young person must be able to progress through the program and toward employability at his own pace.

♦ Services for youth should (1) be provided in the context of a long-term relationship with a caring adult; (2) be comprehensive, following the youth across service systems; (3) be individualized and geared to his developmental needs; (4) address both the relationship needs and the material needs of each participant; and (5) be timely and long term, beginning in the early teens and continuing until youth are 18 to 21 years of age.

SUMMARY OF FINDINGS

The first cohort of young men was recruited into WAY Scholarship at the end of 1984. Every year for the next 10 years, a new cohort of 15 to 20 youths entered the program. These 10 cohorts comprise the treatment group for this study (n=155). In the first 6 years of program operations (1985–1990) youths were recruited into a comparison group (n=76). Both the 10 study cohorts and the 6 comparison cohorts have been followed prospectively through the 5-year program and in some instances beyond. Analyses compared the WAY Scholarship and comparison youths as well as the WAY Scholarship youths and relevant national and New York City data. Some analyses pertain to the full sample of WAY Scholarship participants, while others focus on the youths who stayed with the program for at least 2.5 of the 5 years.

There was low attrition from the program, and those who dropped out were different from those who stayed involved.

Only 24% of the WAY Scholarship youth left within the first half of the 5-year program. Program retention rates improved marginally significantly from the first 6 cohorts (29% attrition) to the last 4 cohorts (16% attrition). Across the 10 cohorts, youth who dropped out of WAY Scholarship were older at enrollment into the program, were discharged from the campus of the Children's Village sooner, and experienced fewer types of early abuse in their lives; they were similar in many important ways including ethnicity, IQ, and behavior problems.

WAY youth gained employment experiences, savings at the end of the program, and were working as adults.

In interviews, youth were very positive about the savings aspect of the program:

★   *The fact that you were saving money was emphasized and that was really cool.*

★   *Every dollar I put in they gave me a dollar for free.*

Youths in cohorts 6 to 10 held on average more than four jobs, with each job lasting on average over 3 months. Youths left jobs for many reasons, and most (71%) were never fired. Youths saved on average over $700 dollars from their WAY Scholarship employment experiences. A subset of cohorts 1 to 6 participants were interviewed as adults in 1997, all of whom had participated in at least 2.5 years of the program. Eighty percent of these young men (21 to 30 years of age) were working, and their reported full-time salaries averaged $22,510.

WAY youth achieved educational success.

WAY Scholarship participants' achievement rates were better than rates for the comparison group, Latinos nationally, New York City black and Latino youth, New York City

Figure 1: Educational Achievement Rates

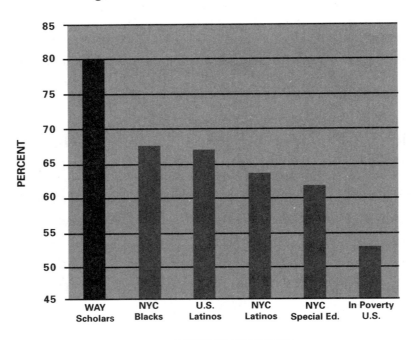

COMPARISON GROUPS

youths in special education, and youths in poverty (Figure 1).[2] These comparisons pertain to 76% of the WAY Scholarship sample who participated in at least half of the 5-year program.

- *At the end of the program—cohorts 1–10:* Eighty-one percent of WAY youth were still in school or had already graduated. This figure pertains to youths who participated for at least 2.5 years (76% of the participants).

- *At the end of the program—WAY versus comparison groups, cohorts 1–6:* For youths who remained involved in WAY or the comparison group (71% for WAY and 80% for the comparison group), the WAY Scholarship youth achievement rate was statistically significantly higher than that of the comparison youth (82% versus 66%).

---

2. The WAY educational achievement rate of 80% is based on the proportion of youths in cohorts 1 to 6 who, at age 21, were high school graduates, had completed a GED, were in a GED program, or were still in school. The national graduation rates are based on U.S. Census data (Federal Interagency Forum on Child and Family Statistics 1999). These graduates include all persons 18 to 24 years of age who received a diploma or an equivalent alternative credential (e.g., the GED). The New York City graduation rates are from the Board of Education (1996) and are based on a three-year follow-up study of the class of 1993. Achievement rates for those 18 to 24 in the general population living below the poverty level in 1997 who had completed high school are reported in Westat (1991).

♦ *At age 21:* Eighty percent of the youth were still in school or had already graduated, and about one-third were enrolled in college. Four of the eight youths who had dropped out of school at the end of the program had reenrolled, and four of the seven youths who had dropped out of college by the end of the program had reenrolled by age 21. It was clear that most of these youths needed more than four years to complete their high school education. Seventy-two percent of those in school at the end of the 5-year program had completed their high school education by age 2 21. These data pertain to youths in cohorts 1 to 6 who participated for at least 2.5 years (71% of the sample).

WAY Scholarship participants prepared for self-sufficiency.

Over 95% of WAY scholars were on a self-sufficiency trajectory at the end of the program (they were either in school, working, or had obtained high school or equivalency degrees). These data pertain to youths in cohorts 1 to 10 who participated in the program for at least 2.5 years (76% of the sample).

WAY Scholarship youths who remained involved in the program had lower adult criminality rates than program dropouts or comparison youth.

Youths who participated in at least 2.5 years of the program had significantly lower adult criminality rates (5%) than youths who left the program before 2.5 years (35%). Youths who participated in at least 2.5 years of the program had marginally significantly lower adult criminality rates (5%) than comparison group youths (15%).

WAY scholars felt positive about their counselors. Most had at least one long-term relationship and worked with counselors of the same gender and ethnicity, which are factors associated with positive outcomes.

Three-fourths of WAY scholars interviewed (cohorts 1 to 6 youths only who had participated in the program for at least 2.5 years) spontaneously reported positive feelings about their counselors—paid, professional mentors—indicating that they played an instrumental role in helping them make the transition from CV to life in the community. A study of youths in cohorts 6 to 10 showed that most worked with counselors of the same gender and same ethnicity for the majority of their involvement in WAY

Scholarship. They averaged 2.5 changes in assigned counselors over the course of the program, and the longest time on average a youth worked with one counselor was almost 3 years. Youths who worked with female counselors had lower end-of-program self-sufficiency and educational attainment, but there was no association with percentage of time working or savings. Similarly, youths who switched counselors less often had greater self-sufficiency and educational attainment at the end of the program, but there was no relationship with savings or percentage of time working.

RECOMMENDATIONS

Youth discharged from foster care need intensive aftercare services.

Youth discharged from foster care are still quite vulnerable, with long-standing family and school difficulties. Many flounder as they make the transition to a less restrictive placement or back home. They need support and guidance to sustain the gains they have made while in care. High reentry rates bear this out. For example, Festinger (1996) found that one-fifth of all discharges from foster care resulted in reentry within two years. Even youth who age out of foster care evidence academic, emotional, and behavioral problems. For example, Blome (1997) found that former foster care youth were more likely to exhibit emotional and behavioral problems than a comparison group. Courtney and Piliavan (1998) also found that youth experienced many practical and emotional problems once discharged from care. The young men who participated in the WAY Scholarship program were no exception. Discharge from care did not represent an end to their mental health, educational, or social support needs. They experienced many financial and emotional hardships in the years following discharge.

In New York, residential treatment costs roughly $50,000 per year, and the average length of stay is two years. For youths who are discharged to their own responsibility, the length of stay is generally much longer. Funding for aftercare in most states, including New York, is nonexistent. Aftercare services, such as those provided by WAY Scholarship, cost roughly $3,000—hardly a steep investment to sustain the gains made during years in expensive out-of-home care. *It is recommended that long-term aftercare services, available for years not months, be provided for adolescents discharged from residential treatment centers.*

Aftercare services should follow youth across service systems.

High-risk youth in general, and young people discharged from foster care in particular, tend to move frequently—among and between relatives and friends and in and out of different service systems. Cook's (1994) follow-up study of youth discharged from care revealed that one-third of youth moved five or more times in the two to four years following discharge. This was certainly true of the WAY Scholarship participants. No matter where a youth was headed—group home, birth family, foster family, Job Corps, or more restrictive level of care—most relocated several times in the years following discharge. Some WAY Scholarship youth moved from the supervision of CV to the care of another agency, while others moved in and out of foster care several times in the ensuing years.

Private funding for the program allowed the WAY Scholarship counselors to follow the youth and provide services, regardless of what other system they entered. This approach stands in stark contrast to the traditional community-based approach in which youth are expected to start over with each relocation or involvement in a new service system. Many adolescents are reluctant to form new relationships, so we need to nurture the good relationships that have been established and allow adults to stay with youth. In that way, no matter what community youth move to, no matter what system they are in, a trusted adult can provide the continuity that links the youth to the services they need. *It is recommended that aftercare staff be given flexibility in funding and in access to youth to provide continuity in care.*

Youth leaving care need long-term counseling and mentoring.

★   *I would like to have had a counselor in college...it might have made a difference in my decision to transfer.*

★   *The low point is when you realize you are own your own. Nobody is there to support you. Nobody is there to push you.*

The idea of offering 5 years of intensive aftercare services to foster care youth was unheard of 15 years ago, when the WAY Scholarship program was developed. It still is. Yet, interviews with the WAY scholars revealed that, for many, 5 years was not enough. Most could have benefited from an even longer-term commitment from the program, one that extended well into their young adulthood. This was true for youth in college who yearned for adult guidance and support as they navigated a new and demanding world. It was true for youth in the working world striving to become responsible adults. It was also true for youth still struggling to overcome a lifetime of family trauma and not yet on a path of self-sufficiency. For many youth, the WAY Scholarship counselor was the most important adult in their lives. For them, the end of the program came too soon. *It is recommended that aftercare services be provided to former foster care youth on a long-term basis, well into their young adulthood.*

Mentors should be paid professionals.

★ *There is this one person in your corner whose total role is to be there to support you during the most crucial times.*

Mentors for this population should be paid professionals with reasonable caseloads (15 to 20 youths) and clearly defined expectations and measures of accountability. Each young person needs to feel that at least one person has a strong stake and interest in his success. For some youth leaving residential treatment, a loving, supportive family member awaits them. Even in these circumstances, the involvement of a mentor is usually welcomed and needed. For the majority of older youth in residential care, there is no one. These young people are often discharged to their own responsibility. The paid professional mentors in the WAY Scholarship program were there to provide them with support, guidance, and caring along the way, from discharge through young adulthood.

The current focus on volunteer mentors for at-risk youth that is sweeping the country is extremely positive, and it is important for many vulnerable youngsters. But for youth discharged from residential treatment, it is probably not enough. Volunteers cannot be expected to go to the extreme lengths that many of the WAY Scholarship counselors had to go to in order to develop and sustain relationships with the program participants. Volunteers cannot be held accountable the same way paid mentors can, and they cannot be expected to be versed in the range of issues and systems relevant to the lives of WAY Scholarship youth. For example, WAY counselors helped youth access housing and mental health services, detected early warning signs of drug use, advocated within the public school system, provided guidance in completing college applications and applications for financial assistance, and so forth. The needs of the youth are too great and the demands on the counselor too many for anyone other than a paid professional to reasonably be expected to do this kind of work, day in and day out, year in and year out. *It is recommended that mentors in programs like WAY be paid professionals who have the time and skills necessary to make a difference in the lives of young people.*

PROGRAMMATIC CHALLENGES

Youth need help preparing for a career.

Young adults not bound for college need the most help in planning for their future, yet they receive the least assistance and face the greatest risks in the job market (Orfield & Paul 1994). This is partly because high school general education alone does not provide adequate preparation for a successful career, and no real guidance system is in place in American high schools for noncollege-bound youth (Mendel 1995). Nationwide, a 1994 survey found that only one-fourth of school guidance counselors spent any real time helping students with career planning. A high school degree is not a guarantee of achieving a stable employment history at a job with a livable wage. Thus, it is no surprise that one-third of all youth with a high school level education fail to find stable employment by the time they are 30 (Osterman 1991, cited in Mendel 1995).

Not all WAY Scholarship youth attended college. The employment histories of the youth interviewed revealed that many went from job to job without actually developing a career path that would ultimately lead to a satisfying and well-paying livelihood. Although some obtained full-time employment with decent wages and health benefits, many had not. They were what the U.S. Department of Labor (1999) refers to as "the stuck, not the skilled." *Thus, a challenge for the WAY Scholarship and similar programs is to help noncollege-bound participants develop career paths that will result in jobs that pay a livable wage.*

Youth need help succeeding in college.

- ★ *College is a whole different ball game.*

- ★ *It is nothing like high school. It is all on you.*

The 20 highest paying professions in this country require at least a bachelor's degree. College graduates on average earn 71% more than high school graduates (U.S. Department of Labor 1999). Attending college is not enough. Graduation is critical. WAY scholars appeared to understand the importance of pursuing postsecondary education. One-fourth at the end of the program and 40% at age 21 had participated in some postsecondary education. Yet, one of the themes that emerged in the interviews with the WAY Scholarship participants was that not all youth enrolled in college graduated.[3] It is important to remember that WAY scholars are not screened into the program based on academic success. Quite the contrary is true. All WAY Scholarship youth were classified as requiring special education and many were years behind in their education at the time of enrollment into WAY.

For most WAY Scholarship participants who attended college, postsecondary education was much harder than they had anticipated, both academically and socially. For many, the start of college overlapped with their "graduation" from the WAY program—either because the youth moved away to attend college or because it coincided with their fifth year in the program. Unfortunately, entering college did not signify that these youth no longer needed the support of their WAY counselors. Quite the opposite was true; many spoke of feeling overwhelmed by the academic demands of their coursework and by the array of choices they had to make on their own. They had to decide which courses to take, how many courses to take each semester, and they had to learn how to balance social and athletic interests with schoolwork. College is a demanding time for any young person, filled with many new experiences and challenges, a time when adult support and guidance are needed.

An additional challenge for the WAY scholars was that, although they were accepted into college, some were not prepared academically to meet the demands of their coursework. They did not have the study skills and discipline nor the foundation of a solid academic high school education to succeed in college (many had achieved general equivalency diplomas, special education degrees, or suffered academically after attending many different high schools). Moreover, many WAY youth in college did not have a home to visit during holidays and other school breaks. Youth over the age of 21 were no longer eligible for services from CV even though they had no other "home." Thus, in addition to the academic stresses WAY scholars faced, holidays and vacations posed both logistical and emotional challenges for these youth. Some stayed temporarily at

---

3. Data are not yet available on college graduation rates of WAY scholars.

their former group homes or came "home" to CV for the holidays. *Thus, a challenge for the WAY program is to determine how best to prepare these young men for a successful college experience. What kinds of supports and assistance do they need so that they can not only attend college but also become college graduates? Many WAY youth are on the path toward success, but even they are in need of continued support as they enter adulthood.*

FUTURE DIRECTIONS

Program Replication

The full WAY program (Levels 1 to 5) and the WAY Scholarship components have been replicated in settings beyond CV. In 1994 CV received a $1.4 million grant from the U.S. Department of Labor for the replication of the WAY Scholarship program in four community-based settings. Results of that four-year effort led to the development of a set of recommendations for the replication of youth employment programs. The full WAY program has also been implemented at Genesis Homes, a HELP housing project in one of the most desolate neighborhoods in New York City. This adaptation of WAY into a housing project complex for former homeless families has proven to be especially promising. HELP has now taken over the project along with the help of a consortium of private funders. In light of the growing interest within and beyond the child welfare community, CV has created a WAY Replication Unit, devoted to overseeing high-quality replications of the WAY program.

Future Research

Much has been learned over the years about how to conceptualize involvement in and outcomes of the WAY program. CV's research department, in collaboration with the WAY Replication Unit, has created a set of common data collection tools for all replications of the WAY program. These tools will allow for a standardized process for describing program participants, level of involvement in the program, and key educational and employment outcomes. In addition, CV will continue to follow the first six cohorts of program participants as older adults.

1

....

Introduction

Adolescents leaving the foster care system—especially those from group care settings—face a multitude of challenges in their transition to adulthood and independence. Many are poor, from ethnic minority backgrounds, and have a history of serious emotional and behavioral problems that led to their placement. The odds of their becoming self-sufficient and productive adults are not in their favor. Thus, The Children's Village (CV) created the Work Appreciation for Youth (WAY) program in 1984 to help youth stay in and graduate from high school and to help them develop work attitudes and skills. WAY, which has been in continuous operation since 1984, has two components: WAY Works, an employment and work ethics program for youth on CV's campus; and WAY Scholarship, an intensive aftercare program for youth leaving residential treatment.

The WAY program has five levels, tailored and sequenced for youth while they live in the residential treatment center (RTC) environment and for four to five years after they are discharged from care. WAY Works, Levels 1 to 4, is the in-treatment component of WAY. Level 5, known as WAY Scholarship, is the highest level of the program and serves a subset of WAY Works boys[1] about to be discharged from care. All youths residing on CV's RTC campus participate in Level 1, performing nonpaid chores within their cottage. In Level 2, youths perform small jobs in their cottage or neighborhood for token payment. In Level 3—for those who are at least 11 years of age and submit an application—youths work in paid jobs at CV's campus worksites. In Level 4—for youths who have succeeded at Level 3—youths work at paid jobs off campus. It is WAY Scholarship (Level 5)—the aftercare component—that is the focus of this study. The goals of the WAY Scholarship program are to provide the ongoing support necessary to help youth develop and sustain positive attitudes toward education and work, to teach young people skills for getting and holding a job, and to help youth plan for their future and acquire a sense of control over their lives. As its name implies, the Work Appreciation

---

1. CV serves a co-educational population in all of its community-based programs and some residential services but only boys in the RTC.

for Youth Scholarship program is a youth employment program. However, it is more than that—it is also a general youth development program, a drop-out prevention program, an independent living program, and a mentoring program.

The five core elements of WAY Scholarship (Level 5) are:

1. long-term, individualized *counseling and mentoring* to help WAY participants meet challenges and solve problems;

2. *educational advocacy and tutoring* to facilitate school success;

3. *work experiences and work ethics* training to enable participants to build work histories and a sense of themselves as workers;

4. *group activities and workshops* to promote a positive peer culture and help youth develop life skills; and

5. *financial incentives* to help youth plan, save, and believe in their futures.

This report begins with an overview of the many factors that place youth at risk for the negative developmental outcomes of educational failure, unemployment and underemployment, and criminality (Chapter 2). The rationale, philosophy, and design of the WAY Scholarship program are described in Chapter 3, followed by a description of the methods and sample of the 15-year, 10-cohort study of the WAY Scholarship program (Chapter 4). Findings regarding employment, education, self-sufficiency, and criminality are presented in Chapters 5 through 9. Chapter 10 explores how WAY scholars felt about their counselors and considers whether "mentoring" was associated with positive outcomes. The discussion (Chapter 11) suggests directions for future research as well as lessons learned and programmatic challenges.

2

Theoretical Background

Demographic Risk Factors for School Failure, Unemployment, and Criminality

In today's increasingly technological society, staying in and doing well in school are critical for economic and social well-being (Catterall 1987; Levin 1983; Schorr 1989; William T. Grant Foundation 1988). Young adults who leave school before graduating face a number of potential hardships. Compared with high school graduates, relatively more dropouts are unemployed (22%), and those dropouts who do find work earn less money than high school graduates (U.S. Department of Education 1996). According to census statistics, high school dropouts earn an average of $15,000 per year, while high school graduates earn an average of $22,000; and college graduates earn an average of $38,000 (U.S. Department of Labor 1998). School failure is also associated with criminal behavior (Thornberry et al. 1985), unemployment (Rumberger 1995), and "underclass" status (Ricketts & Sawhill 1988). According to 1995 statistics, high school dropouts comprised nearly half the heads of households on welfare and a similar percentage of the prison population (Schwartz 1995). Thus, the costs of school failure are high for the individual, for his or her family, and for the community.

The importance of a successful high school education cannot be overstated as a predictor of legitimate employment. This is even truer today than a generation ago. Youth today face a more challenging economic future than ever before. Competition in the labor market is more intense, the number and type of career paths that can be pursued without postsecondary education have become more limited, and the earning prospects of young wage earners have declined dramatically. According to Sum and Heliotis (cited in American Youth Policy Forum 1997), in 1995 the majority of young adults (17 to 24 years of age) who were not in school (and who had not earned a high school degree) were experiencing severe difficulty obtaining full-time employment with adequate wages. Earnings for young people who left school before graduating have fallen by more than 25% over the past three decades (Center for Human Resources 1993).

Despite the importance of school success, too many youth are at risk for educational failure. Several risk factors have been well documented in the literature (Rumberger 1995), including three family-level variables: ethnicity, income, and single-parent households. For example, in 1992 dropout rates among 16- to 24-year-olds were 8% for white youth, but 14% for black youth, and 29% for Latino youth (McMillen et al. 1993). Special education classification is also strongly associated with poor academic performance and risk of dropping out of school (Rylance 1997; Wagner & Blackorby 1996). According to data from the National Longitudinal Transition Study of Special Education Students (NLTS), 38% of youth with disabilities dropped out of high school (Wagner & Blackorby 1996). Other analyses found that among 664 18- to 27-year-old youth identified as having severe emotional disturbances, barely half (50%) completed their high school education (Rylance 1997). Furthermore, exposure to multiple risk factors can dramatically increase the likelihood that youth will exhibit poor school performance (Luster & McAdoo 1994). Thus, being poor, black or Latino, living in a single-parent household, and requiring special education dramatically increase the risk for school failure.

The strong link between school success and employment means that the very populations most at risk for school failure are the same youth at risk for eventual unemployment and underemployment. Thus, youth who grow up poor tend to do poorly in school and therefore tend to remain economically disadvantaged as adults. Their children are raised in poverty, continuing the cycle of educational failure and unemployment (Smith et al. 1992).

In addition to the effects of poverty on life outcomes, disadvantaged youth face what researchers have called a "web of mutually reinforcing circumstances and behaviors" that makes a successful attachment to the labor market extremely difficult (Kazis & Kopp 1997). Such circumstances include the deterioration of the labor market in urban communities, overwhelming personal and family issues that would distract even the most dedicated student and worker, and a mismatch between employer demands and the skills of entry-level workers. Indeed, lack of skills and preparation for the workforce has been cited as one of the most important reasons for the failure of youth to obtain long-term employment (Holzer 1996).

Lack of preparation for the transition from school to work is problematic for many minority youth. In general, high school students are ill-prepared for the world of work, a problem that is exacerbated by high school guidance counselors' exclusive focus on postsecondary education. According to an Educational Testing Service survey, almost half of all students never talked to a guidance counselor about possible future occupations (Chapman & Katz 1981). These noncollege-bound youth received little or no support or guidance in making a successful transition to the work force, often leading to a period of "floundering" as these young adults entered the labor market. As Orfield and Paul (cited in Mendel 1995) noted, "Students not bound for college need the most help, receive the least assistance, are equipped with the most limited information, and experience the greatest risks in the job market." Osterman (cited in Mendel 1995) identified minority youth among several groups for whom this chaotic entry into the labor market is particularly harmful. According to Kazis (1993), the employment picture for young black and Latino youth who do not make it to college is so bleak as to constitute a serious school-to-work crisis.

Access to and identification with adults who have developed labor force attachments are also critical to an adolescent's successful entry into employment. Yet Farrell (1990) found that at-risk minority youth have limited involvement with gainfully employed adult role models. He found that their understanding of the process of getting and maintaining employment was often limited, unrealistic, and inaccurate. Taken together, these data paint a picture of minority youth who are more likely to fail in school and less likely to build a foundation upon which to create an adult life in which they can support themselves and their families.

Educational failure and lack of success in the labor market are two key correlates of eventual adult criminal behavior. Thus, poor minority youth are also at high risk of becoming involved in illegal activities. Moreover, ethnic minority status itself is associated with disproportionate involvement with the criminal justice system. For example, it has been well documented that police officers are more likely to view minorities as suspects than nonminorities.[1] In a 1990 report, the Sentencing Project (Mauer 1990) found that almost one in four black males in the 20 to 29 age group was under some form of criminal justice supervision. Updated figures suggest that nearly one in three black males in that age group are under criminal justice supervision on any given day—in prison, jail, or on probation or parole (Mauer & Huling 1995). Among those in out-of-home care, black males are five times more likely to be in the juvenile justice system than white males (Fletcher 1997).

---

1. Such policing affects many minorities. In *Race Matters*, West (1993) describes being stopped on false charges of trafficking cocaine when he was a young professor. For a good discussion on the common practice of discriminatory policing, see Kennedy (1992).

Poor minority youth are also at risk for criminal involvement because of the neighborhoods in which they are raised. Indeed, crime is largely an urban phenomenon among young males (Phillips et al. 1972). Areas of concentrated urban poverty tend to have disproportionately high crime rates (Sampson 1997). As noted by Anderson (1997, p. 1):

> The inclination to violence springs from the circumstances of life among the ghetto poor—the lack of jobs that pay a living wage, the stigma of race, the fallout from rampant drug use and drug trafficking, and the resulting alienation and lack of hope for the future.

Foster Care Placement as a Risk Factor for Negative Outcomes

Youth in foster care are at especially high risk for negative life outcomes. In addition to the lingering effects of their early environments (e.g., single-parent households, poverty), youth in foster care are also at risk due to the factors that led to their out-of-home placement. These include physical and sexual abuse; physical and emotional neglect; abandonment; and parental mental illness, incarceration, and substance abuse. Due to these early life traumas, youth in foster care represent one of the most at-risk populations in the country. As Fanshel (1992, p. 55) has stated, "Foster care children are probably among the most disadvantaged among the larger group of children in the United States who have been deprived of the basic essentials of normal childhood." He describes the chronic exposure to unusual degrees of family violence, abuse, and neglect and concludes that "children from such families represent a major potential source of tomorrow's criminals."

A recent study conducted in Sacramento County, California, by the Child Welfare League of America (CWLA 1997) confirmed the relationship between foster care placement and subsequent criminal activity. Researchers found that the arrest rate among children referred to child welfare for abuse or neglect was 67 times greater than the arrest rate among children not known to the child welfare system. A recent survey of prisoners found that 14% of jail inmates had lived in a foster home or agency at some point in their lives (Harlow 1998).

Youth in foster care are also at risk for low educational attainment and unemployment or underemployment. Research suggests that school disruptions and difficult life circumstances combine to impede the educational and employment success of these youth. For example, Blome (1997) found that more than twice as many foster care youth had changed schools three or more times since fifth grade than youth not in foster care. Only 15% of the foster care youth in Blome's study were enrolled in college preparatory classes, half spent less than three hours per week on homework, and 37% had dropped out of high school.

Adolescents discharged from foster care face even greater risks for negative life outcomes than younger children leaving the system, because fewer than 20% will return home and fewer than 5% will be adopted (Cook 1988). Adolescents are likely to have emotional problems upon entering care and to experience difficulty when leaving care (Mech 1988). Follow-up studies of adolescents in foster care paint a dismal picture of youth ill-prepared for self-sufficient and productive lives. The Wisconsin study of youth aging out of out-of-home care, *Foster Youth Transition to Adulthood: Outcomes 12 to 18 Months After Leaving Out-of-Home Care,* followed 141 youth 18 months after discharge (Courtney & Piliavin 1998). These researchers found that life after foster care posed many challenges for 17- to 18-year-old youth. Thirty-seven percent had not yet completed high school. Ten percent had been homeless at some time in the preceding 12 to 18 months; 32% had received public assistance, and 42% had difficulty obtaining medical care. These data are consistent with Roman and Wolfe's (1997) finding that almost 40% of homeless individuals are former foster care youth.

Courtney and Piliavin (1998, p. 10) also asked about youths' feelings of preparedness for independent living. About one-quarter to one-third of the interviewed youth reported feeling ill-prepared in several skill areas. For example, one-third reported feeling not at all or not very well prepared to obtain a job or manage money. About one-third reported feeling similarly ill-prepared to obtain housing. Over one-fourth of the sample reported not feeling ready to live on their own. The authors concluded that a "large majority of the participants experienced situations seriously dangerous to their well-being or otherwise indicative of an unsuccessful transition to independence."

Festinger (1983, pp. 298–299) also found educational and employment lags among young adults who had been in foster care as adolescents. At the time of discharge, one-third had not yet graduated from high school, and nearly 43% of the males had been suspended from school in the postdischarge period. Particularly poor outcomes were experienced by youth discharged from group or institutional care, as opposed to family-based foster homes. As Festinger points out:

> It was a particularly difficult time for those who left group facilities since, unlike many from foster homes, they were obliged to leave their places of residence, which made the transition into the community more abrupt. But

regardless of whether they were discharged from group or foster family care, the road was most difficult for those who had to fend for themselves because of limited or tenuous ties to adults in the community.

At a time when other adolescents are developing independent living skills (ILS) under the guidance and support of families, youth in foster care are somehow expected to become self-sufficient despite the fact that they have been in a dependent living situation that did not provide them with the opportunities to practice and develop those very skills (Cook 1988). North et al. (1988, p. 577) summarized the many challenges to achieving ILS for foster care youth:

> Young people must accumulate an enormous amount of learning to function independently in our society. For most adolescents this learning occurs informally and experientially in the family setting over a period of years. In contrast, many foster care youth may have come from a dysfunctional family where there were limited opportunities to learn in the typical way. Many youth experience multiple placements, which further reduces the range of opportunities for informal learning.

Blome (1997, p. 42) summarized the plight of foster care youth leaving the system in a similar manner:

> It is a curious reality that society's most vulnerable youth, those who have suffered abuse or neglect and have never known consistent, permanent, nurturing adult relationships, are asked to be self-sufficient at a time when other youth are still receiving parental support in college or are experimenting with their first jobs from within the safe confines of a family.

Despite the many difficulties youth leaving foster care face, the child welfare system offers no postdischarge transitional living services. Rather, the focus of child welfare services has been on permanency placement and family reunification as an end in itself. With the passage of P.L. 99–272, the Independent Living Initiative, there has been attention given to developing and implementing "independent living services" but, in most states, even these services end at the point of discharge from the system. The law authorized funds for states beginning in fiscal year 1987 to establish and carry out programs to assist youth at 16 years of age and older to make the transition to independent living. As of today, all states have created such plans, with New York's being one of the most comprehensive. New York's plan includes the "requirement" of case supervision until youth reach age 21. Yet, it does not allocate funding for the postdischarge phase. Even with the advent of P.L. 99–272, very little attention has been paid to the aftercare component of independent living services. Nearly all services to enhance ILS are provided while youth are still in care. According to Westat (1989), aftercare services are most often neglected by agencies, whether they are stipulated or not. Based on the difficulty some youth have had after discharge from care, Mallon (1998, p. 6) concluded that:

> The need for transitional programming for these adolescents extends beyond the age at which they are discharged from out-of-home care. Ongoing relationships with instrumental and effective supports have to be developed for young people leaving care. Variation in their skill levels demands that aftercare services be highly individualized. Long-term support may be necessary.

3

The WAY Program Developed at The Children's Village

CV serves some of the most troubled youth in the New York City child welfare system. The youth residing in CV's RTC—as opposed to foster homes—are an extremely disadvantaged subset of foster care children. Only 4% of the youth in the New York City Child Welfare system are deemed disturbed enough to warrant placement in an RTC. Nearly all are poor, from minority ethnic backgrounds, and from some of the most impoverished areas of the Greater New York Metropolitan area. But beyond that, most of the children have had multiple prior out-of-home placements and hospitalizations, and all have severe emotional or behavioral problems. The majority of the children are the victims of family upheaval and serious neglect, trauma, or abuse (on admission 70% of the youth have histories of adjudicated neglect and 40% have histories of adjudicated abuse), with many also manifesting neurological or biochemical impairments that underlie their emotional problems.

To increase the chances that older youth discharged from CV's RTC would have a chance in life, CV created and implemented a comprehensive program to teach youth work ethics, to provide youth with opportunities to learn how to work, to encourage youth to stay in school, and to save and plan for their future. The WAY program, initiated in 1984, was also designed to prepare youth to transition from residential treatment back to their families and communities, to either less restrictive settings or to independent living. Thus, WAY included both an in-care component and an intensive aftercare component. Staff at CV believed that helping youth stay in school and complete high school was of paramount importance, especially for low-income, urban, minority youth with a history of emotional and behavioral problems. Only by doing so would these extremely at-risk youth have a chance to sustain whatever mental health gains they made while in care and to become viable candidates for jobs in the labor market. It was within this context that the WAY program was developed.

CV created the WAY program to teach work ethics prior to discharge and to provide intensive supportive services to youth after they leave CV in order to increase the chances that they would stay in school and be firmly planted on a path toward self-sufficiency. From the beginning, the WAY program incorporated features that have since been identified by researchers and policymakers as key to successful youth programming (Kazis & Kopp 1997; Walker 1997). Researchers at Manpower Demonstration Research Corporation, a leader in the evaluation of employment programs, concluded, "The two most important elements of a stable labor market experience are a sound basic education and a combination of work habits, attitudes, and skills" (MDRC 1983, p. 16). It is just this combination that is at the heart of the WAY program.

The full WAY program instituted at CV has five levels, tailored and sequenced for youth while they live in the RTC environment and after they are discharged from care. Levels 1 to 4, WAY Works, is the in-treatment component of WAY. Level 5, known as WAY Scholarship, is targeted for a subset of youth who are about to be discharged from care.

- ◆ All youth residing on CV's RTC campus participate in Level 1, performing nonpaid chores within their cottage (15 youth live in each of 21 cottages).

- ◆ Level 2 youth perform small jobs in their cottage or neighborhood for token payment.

- ◆ Level 3 youth work in paid jobs at one of CV's campus employment sites (e.g., computer lab, greenhouse, youth newspaper). These jobs require formal applications and regular performance evaluations.

- ◆ Level 4 youth work at paid jobs off campus (e.g., local hospitals, stores, day care centers).

- ◆ It is the WAY Scholarship component (Level 5) that is the focus of this study. The goals of the WAY Scholarship program are to solidify the skills and attitudes learned in WAY Works, especially maintaining a positive attitude toward education and work, teaching young people skills for getting and holding a job, and helping participants plan for their future and acquire a sense of control over their lives.

Key Assumptions Underlying the Development of the WAY Scholarship Program

- ♦ Employability and the acquisition of basic education skills are linked.

- ♦ The development of work ethics (e.g., self-discipline, cooperation, responsibility) and a work history at a young age will supply youth with skills and attitudes that can help them obtain and maintain employment at an older age.

- ♦ Program components must be developmentally appropriate and work experiences must be carefully sequenced.

- ♦ A young person must be able to progress through the program and toward employability at his own pace.

Based on those assumptions, honed through years of working with a subset of the most troubled children in the child welfare system, the WAY Scholarship program was developed to include the following principles and elements.

Core Principles of the WAY Scholarship Program

- ♦ Services for youth are provided in the context of a long-term relationship with a caring adult.

- ♦ Services for youth are comprehensive and follow the youth across systems.

- ♦ Services are individualized, specifically geared to the developmental needs of each teenager.

- ♦ Services are intended to address both the relationship needs and the material needs of each participant.

- ♦ Services are timely and long term, beginning with preteen youngsters and continuing for 5 years, until they are 18 to 21 years of age.

Five Core Elements of the WAY Scholarship Model

There are five core elements to the WAY Scholarship program: (1) mentoring and counseling, (2) educational advocacy, (3) work experiences, (4) group activities, and (5) financial incentives. How the programmatic elements were incorporated into the WAY Scholarship program is described followed by the rationale for each of these elements.

Long-Term, Individualized Counseling and Mentoring to Help WAY Participants Meet Challenges and Solve Problems

The WAY Scholarship program offered at-risk youth an opportunity to participate in an intensive, individualized, long-term counseling and mentoring relationship. Once enrolled in the WAY Scholarship program, each scholar was assigned a paid, professional WAY counselor with whom he could develop a relationship that formed the core of the WAY experience. The WAY counselor was the essential ingredient in the delivery of the service, ensuring that youths received advocacy, information, encouragement, work ethics education, counseling, and other services as needed to succeed in school and on the job. The counselor was to provide personal and intensive emotional support and practical guidance at every step of the way in the youth's young adulthood. Counselors were to be coaches, cheerleaders, surrogate parents, advocates, teachers, and friends. Most important, they aimed to "hang in there" with each youth no matter how far off track he strayed. In fact, when a youth was most troubled was exactly the time when the counselor was most needed, conveying the very important message that the counselor would never give up on him. In contrast with the current movement for volunteer mentors (e.g., Mech et al. 1995), the WAY Scholarship program hired and trained paid professional mentors. It was believed that hiring professional staff would increase the likelihood that mentors would be able to make a long-term commitment to the youth.

In the past decade, mentoring programs for disadvantaged children and adolescents have received serious attention as a promising approach to enrich young people's lives, meet their need for positive adult contact, and provide one-on-one support and advocacy for those who need it (Grossman 1999; Grossman & Garry 1997). Evaluation of the nation's most well known and widely implemented mentoring program for youth, Big Brothers/Big Sisters, revealed a positive effect of mentoring on youth development (Tierney & Grossman 1995). Youth with mentors were 46% less likely to start using drugs, 52% less likely to skip school, and 33% less apt to engage in violence than their peers randomly selected to participate in the control group. Qualities of the mentoring relationship found to be important were the high level of contact and the level of support provided to the youth. According to a Public/Private Ventures review of several mentoring programs, effective programs screen mentors, provide training especially regarding limit-setting and communication, and provide intensive support and supervision to the mentors (Roaf et al. 1994). They concluded that the research presented definite positive evidence that mentoring programs can create and support caring relationships between adults and youth, resulting in a wide range of tangible benefits. Further, mentoring has been viewed as a viable strategy for working with youth in the foster care system (Mech et al. 1995).

Educational Advocacy and Tutoring to Facilitate School Success

Youth in residential group foster care have many educational needs and may need nonparental adults to be educational advocates. The WAY Scholarship program was based on the premise that each student needs at least one adult to be highly invested in his educational success, to have high expectations, to provide concrete assistance, and to be his ally in dealing with the educational bureaucracy. In the program the WAY Scholarship counselor played this role. The counselor was to monitor the youth's educational progress, provide tutoring services if needed, speak with school guidance counselors when difficulties arose, and assist the youth in selecting appropriate classes, essentially shepherding the youth through the secondary (and sometimes postsecondary) educational process. Whenever possible, this role was carried out with the parent or guardian. WAY Scholarship counselors were also expected to assist parents in becoming more invested in their adolescent's education and to advocate for the needs of WAY Scholarship participants.

Research has documented the importance of adult involvement in the educational process for students' school success (Epstein 1995). Cumulative evidence from the extant research base suggests the importance of several specific types of parent involvement activities, including high expectations and moderate levels of parental support (Kurdek et al. 1995). Although schools are expected to provide the majority of the structured learning experiences for school-aged children, parents and other significant adults play a critical role overseeing the student's educational progress. Parents are expected to monitor homework; to ensure that the youth is in an appropriate educational setting to meet his emotional, behavioral, and academic needs; and to identify and access appropriate external resources as needed. It is the parent's job to intervene if the youth is having difficulty. Principals and teachers expect parents to take on this role, and most parents understand that it is their job to do so (Baker 1997a and 1997b).

Work Experiences and Work Ethics Training to Enable Participants to Build Work Histories and a Sense of Themselves as "Workers"

The WAY Scholarship program offered youth employment experience. In the WAY model, this was accomplished initially through worksites on CV's campus (during Levels 1 to 4 and the first six months of their participation in WAY Scholarship while they still were residing on the campus) and in jobs the youth obtained in the community. It was expected that through these early employment experiences, youth would develop concrete knowledge of what it means to work, would begin to acquire a self-image as "someone who works" (as opposed to someone who hangs out or tries to "get over"), and would develop work ethics (e.g., showing up for work on time, being pleasant and agreeable regardless of personal distractions).

The WAY Scholarship work experiences were designed to build on the work experiences youth obtained while in WAY Works. For example, Levels 2 and 3 of the WAY program[1] were developed to mimic a "real world" employment situation, with attendant application procedures, work rules, and guidelines for dismissal and promotion to the next level of WAY. Employment supervisors evaluated each youngster's job performance at the campus worksites, and the WAY Scholarship counselor was in regular contact with each youth as he obtained employment off campus. Job opportunities were sought for youth, and referrals were provided for regular work, subsidized work, or internships as part of the progression to regular, independently secured employment. It was believed that expecting youth to "earn" and "deserve" their job promoted self-worth and a sense of purpose based on good performance.

In order to be selected for WAY Scholarship, youths must have already participated in WAY Works employment and workshops. Once in WAY Scholarship, youths worked at Level 3 jobs on the campus, Level 4 jobs in the community near CV, and Level 4 jobs in the community to which they were discharged.

CV's Level 3 Worksites
Youth who worked at Level 3 jobs not only had to apply for the job (with written and oral interview components), but also had to maintain a high level of employee attendance and competence in order to keep their jobs. Youths were evaluated on a regular

---

1. Level 2 entailed odd jobs for pay in and around the cottage, and Level 3 entailed formal employment at a CV WAY worksite.

basis and received promotions or demotions based on their performance. Youth who received unfavorable reviews were referred for employment counseling and refresher workshops. In this way, youths were taught skills and behaviors important for adult employment success.

There were six different WAY Level 3 worksites on the grounds of CV: (1) the computer bus, (2) *C.V. News* (youth-run newspaper), (3) grounds, (4) maintenance, (5) the Village store, and (6) the woodshop. In addition, some youth worked in various departments on campus such as in food service or in the warehouse.

♦ *Computer Bus:* The computer bus was a mobile vehicle outfitted as a computer lab station with state-of-the-art computers and educational and recreational software programs. Youth who worked at the computer lab first learned a range of computer skills and then learned to teach these skills to other boys on CV's campus and to people at community sites to which the computer bus traveled. In addition to the standard Level 3 requirements, in order to work on the computer bus, youths also had to complete a 10-week course in computer skills, for which they had to pay to attend. Once they completed the workshop, they had to pass a test. At this worksite, boys had to dress formally in white shirts, black pants, dress shoes, and a tie, learning how to present a professional appearance and demeanor. When on the bus, youths at this worksite taught others how to load, edit, and save word processing documents, as well as how to make banners and greeting cards. They taught basic computer skills and helped others troubleshoot and solve computer hardware and software problems.

♦ *C.V. News:* This worksite was an internal newsletter prepared by CV residents for their peers. C.V. News reported on campus-wide events and news, including descriptions of celebrities who came to the campus and reports on cottage fundraisers, sports, and club events. WAY youth at this site functioned as reporters, writers, and assistants. As reporters they attended campus events in order to gather information for writing a story. Youth who worked at *C.V. News* also learned how a newsletter is put together, laid out, and distributed.

♦ *Grounds and Greenhouse:* At this Level 3 worksite, youth learned how to maintain the grounds of CV's campus. Duties included raking grass and flowerbeds, removing weeds, and propagating plants in the greenhouse as well as performing other greenhouse operations. Youth who worked on the grounds also participated in preparing special projects for sale during the holidays and for crafts shows or other campus events. In addition, each spring the greenhouse sold perennial plants and flowers.

♦ *Village Store:* The Village Store was centrally located on the campus in its own building and was open to CV residents, staff, and visitors during after-school hours, five days a week. The store sold a range of snack items including a wide variety of drinks, chips, and candy along with balloons, comic books, posters, and other fun activities. Youth who worked at this site learned personal hygiene in the food service business, proper handling of perishable foods, customer relations, inventory monitoring, familiarization of the menu, and cash register skills (e.g., making change, controlling customer flow). Typical daily tasks included opening the store, cleaning the grounds of litter, checking stock, and opening the cash register. During hours of operation youths monitored stock, waited on customers, and managed the cash register. At closing they cleaned the area, rectified sales and revenue, and closed out the cash register.

♦ *Woodshop:* The woodshop was located in a nonresidential cottage on the grounds of the campus. Youths who worked there learned woodworking craftsmanship. They built items for sale in the Village Store and at local crafts fairs. They learned wood sanding, wood staining, painting, and how to use hand tools and other machinery. Workers helped build signs, bird houses, shelves, and bookends; and they worked on other campus special projects and requests.

Off-Campus Level 4 Worksites

Once boys successfully mastered Level 3 work, they were eligible to apply for a variety of Level 4 employment positions. Level 4 of the WAY Scholarship program provided youth with opportunities to gain employment experiences off CV's campus, including internships and part-time jobs in various small local businesses or in departments of larger businesses. Youth had to be at least 15 years of age and have satisfactory experience in a Level 3 job. In addition, boys had to have satisfactory grades, demonstrate positive behavior in their cottage, and be recommended for a Level 4 position. Examples of Level 4 jobs included administrative assistant, dietary aide or maintenance assistant at the Dobbs Ferry Hospital, assistant at a print shop, recreation assistant at a local nursing home, assistant at a flower shop, attendant at a service station, and helper at a local delicatessen. Once discharged from CV's campus, all WAY scholars were to work at jobs in the community to which they were discharged. They were to find their own employment situations with the guidance and support of the WAY Scholarship counselor.

Providing minority youth with opportunities to develop employability skills is critical for enhancing youth employment, and ultimately, adult employment. Successful employment is based not only on academic skills, but also on what has been termed "employability skills" (Imel 1993), including how to search for a job and how to demonstrate appropriate work-related characteristics and attitudes (adhering to employer's schedules, getting along with work mates, and working on a team). These skills are typically not taught in the classroom. Rather, they are acquired through apprenticeships and internships available to many middle-class youth who have access to employers through their parents and other key adults in their lives. Low-income youth typically acquire these skills and attitudes through youth employment experiences. It is through such experiences that youth develop a sense of industry and identity as a worker (Vondracek 1993). Thus, for low-income youth, early work experiences create the foundation for future employment. Unemployment in the teenage years is highly predictive of subsequent unemployment (MDRC 1983; Stern 1997). This relationship has also been documented specifically for youth leaving foster care (Courtney & Piliavin 1998).

Yet, the labor market situation of black teenagers is extremely grim (Holzer 1996). The Bureau of Labor Statistics recently reported that the unemployment rate for African American teenagers was 40% (U.S. Department of Labor 1998). These youth do not have access to the very experiences that will provide them with a foundation for subsequent employment. Thus, a significant percentage of the workforce is hard-pressed to meet even the minimum requirements of employability because they lack the very experiences that will teach them what it means to be a worker (Burnett 1992).

Group Activities and Workshops to Promote a Positive Peer Culture and Help Youth Develop Life Skills

While on campus, WAY scholars met regularly with others in the program for group sessions and workshops in work ethics and life skills training. Topics included: job search skills, career planning, social responsibility, citizen rights, decisionmaking, and health education. The work ethics curriculum explored through discussion, role play, videos, exercises, and creative arts projects issues such as dependability, productivity, and the ability to take supervision and get along with others—what the National Alliance of Business considers "work maturity." Once discharged from care, those themes were to become part of the regular counseling relationship between the WAY counselor and the scholar in the real world. A constant "slow drip" process of teaching work and life skills was to continue for the full five years of the program.

The WAY Scholarship awards and induction dinners, held annually in the ballroom of a New York City hotel, were attended by WAY scholars and their families and friends, as well as New York City notables such as politicians and journalists. The dinners celebrated the achievements of WAY scholars and communicated to those youngsters how important their achievements were to their families and to society at large. Graduates of WAY Scholarship and those in their later years of the program inducted the new, younger scholars in a ceremony that expressed the idea that those selected were special, that they had been chosen for membership in a very important "club." Despite the fact that nearly every youth who was eligible and expressed even the most tentative interest in WAY Scholarship participated in the program, the celebrations (and other activities) were designed to solidify their interest, inspire greater interest, and provide a positive peer culture and a sense of "belonging" to something special.

Financial Incentives to Help Youth Plan, Save, and Believe in their Futures

WAY Scholarship offered matched savings whereby youths who saved received up to $500 per year in matching funds to be used toward further education or training upon completion of high school. The matched savings program was intended to help the youth believe that they had a future and to teach them to set longer term goals, plan for the future, and save. WAY Scholarship further supplemented these savings by guaranteeing $1,000 for each year of college or up to 2 years for job training. Nonmatched accounts were also made available to youth for personal spending. As part of their contract to participate in WAY Scholarship, all youth agreed to work part-time and to save part of their earnings.

Most poor youth do not have savings for college. Indeed, many low-income youth do not even have savings accounts to accumulate money for personal items that cost more than the cash they have on hand. CV staff believed that, without strong incentives, many WAY Scholarship youth (all of whom were teenagers) would not save for their future because of their impulsive spending habits and keen desire for the latest music, clothes, and accessories. Encouraging youth to save, it was felt, could help them develop a sense of accomplishment. Matching savings increased the positive benefits of saving by speeding up the process of accumulation and by demonstrating in a very concrete way that adults had faith in them and in their ability to achieve educational goals.

The WAY Scholarship Program's Place in the Context of Other Youth Development and Employment Programs

The WAY Scholarship program consists of the five core elements described in this chapter: counseling, educational advocacy, work ethics and employment experiences, group activities, and financial incentives. Although unique in its particular configuration of program components, the WAY program shares features of other youth employment and youth development programs such as the Job Corps, Youth Incentive Entitlement Pilot Project, YouthBuild, and the Quantum Opportunities Program (QOP). A unique challenge for the WAY program was the implementation of its services for the extremely high-risk youths leaving the most restrictive level of care in the child welfare system. Thus, WAY incorporated an unusually long aftercare component, as much as five years, which is its most distinguishing characteristic. Other programs have taken slightly different approaches with many common elements.

By far the most extensive federal employment initiative developed, the Job Corps program provides 12 months of intensive basic education, vocational skills, and support services to participants in a residential setting. Evaluation of this intensive youth employment program has revealed positive effects. For example, Schochet et al. (2000) compared Job Corps youth and comparison youth 30 months after enrollment into the study. They found that after an average of 8 months of participation, Job Corps youth gained significant academic and vocational experiences and showed an 11% gain in weekly earnings. Today Job Corps is the nation's largest residential education and training program for disadvantaged youth operating 111 centers in 46 states.

Youth Incentive Entitlement Pilot Project (YIEPP) is based on the premise that at-risk youth want to work and will gain positive benefits from employment experiences. In the YIEPP demonstration project, eligible youth were guaranteed full-time employment during the summer and part-time employment during the school year as long as they maintained satisfactory academic performance. The program evaluation focused on participating youth in four pilot programs and comparison youth from similar cities without the YIEPP program. Results revealed that participating youth earned more than their comparison peers both during and after the program, although for black teens there was no effect on school enrollment rates (Farkas et al. 1984).

The use of long-term mentors is key to the QOP, a $1 million experiment financed by the Ford Foundation. The original 4-year program was operated in four American cities and offered intensive educational assistance, community service, and developmental activities to at-risk youth. QOP services were provided by adult mentors to AFDC (Aid to Families with Dependent Children) families with children in the 9th grade for 4 years. Hahn (1994) conducted a random assignment evaluation of 100 participants at 4 sites. At the end of 4 years, only 23% of the participants had dropped out of school, compared with half the control group. Success varied by site but was evident in all four programs and was attributed to the constancy of the adult mentoring across the length of the program. Originally funded by the Ford Foundation, currently the Department of Labor is supporting program expansion.

Funded by a team of private national foundations, the YouthBuild demonstration provided at-risk minority males with work experiences and educational assistance. The program operated on a 12-month cycle and offered unemployed and out-of-school 16- to 24-year-olds job training, counseling, and leadership opportunities through the construction and rehabilitation of affordable housing in their communities. Reporting on the effect of program participation on 177 participants, Ferguson and Clay (1996, p. 20) found that after 6 months of services, 20% of the youth obtained their general equivalency diploma (GED). They concluded that because of the more at-risk nature of the population served (all males), the YouthBuild program "is probably distinctive in its capacity to retain and serve this important group." The U.S. Department of Housing and Urban Development has supported the scaling up of YouthBuild to 145 sites across the country.

Based on the evaluations of these and similar programs, researchers in the field of youth employment and youth development have concluded that certain programmatic features are key for success. These features include adult support, creative forms of learning, strong connections to the workplace, ongoing support and follow-up, and conceptualizing youth as resources (American Youth Policy Forum 1997). Walker (1997) developed a similar set of principals for effective youth programming, including the importance of one special adult relationship for each youth, a strong connection to employers, creating a desire in youth to improve their skills, long-term support and assistance, connections to other support services in the community, creation of an atmosphere of involvement and service, and motivational techniques. The WAY Scholarship program incorporated many if not all of the elements considered critical for successful youth development and youth employment programs.

4

The WAY Study

The WAY Scholarship program has been the focus of intensive longitudinal program evaluation since its inception. This chapter presents the methods of the 10-cohort, 15-year study.

Methods

Funding to develop and launch a longitudinal prospective study of the WAY Scholarship program was provided by the private donors who funded the program. From the beginning, researchers worked closely with program staff to develop recruitment procedures, design the study, and oversee data collection. In 1994 CV's administrative offices caught fire, resulting in extensive damage to the research office and research documentation. The research department was able to recoup much of the lost data, but some agency files that were important to the study could not be restored. In addition, the design of the study evolved over time as changes were made in staffing and in the field of program evaluation. Thus, some data originally not collected were later deemed necessary but were no longer available. Therefore, some analyses were tailored to accommodate missing information. Despite these challenges, we believe that sufficient data were available to address most of the primary research questions.

Design

At the end of 1984, the first cohort of young men was recruited into the WAY Scholarship program. Every year for the next 10 years, a new cohort of approximately 15 to 20 youth entered WAY Scholarship. These 10 cohorts of program participants comprise the treatment group for this study (n=155). In the first 6 years of program operations (1985–1990), a group of youths similar to the program participants were recruited as a comparison group (n=76). Both the 10 study cohorts and the 6 comparison cohorts have been followed prospectively through the 5-year program and in some instances beyond.

Some analyses compare cohorts 1 to 6 WAY Scholarship (n=93) with cohorts 1 to 6 from the comparison group (n=76). Other data are presented for WAY scholars alone and include cohorts 1 to 6 (n=93), cohorts 6 to 10 (n=78), or cohorts 1 to 10 (n=155), depending on availability of data. In some analyses, a subset of WAY scholars from cohorts 1 to 6 who participated in at least 2.5 years of the program (71% of the enrollees) are looked at more closely (n=66). In some analyses, these 66 youth are compared with the subset (80%) of comparison group youth who did not drop out of the comparison group. Table 1 presents an overview of the sample size for each cohort and for the various subgroups of interest.

Table 1: WAY Scholarship and Comparison Group Enrollment (by Cohort)

Cohort	Year Enrolled (January)	WAY Enrollment	WAY ≥ 2.5 Years	WAY < 2.5 Years	Comparison Enrollment
1	1985	15	8	7	15
2	1986	17	14	3	14
3	1987	15	12	3	13
4	1988	16	8	8	9
5	1989	14	11	3	7
6	1990	16	13	3	18
Subtotal (1–6)	*1985–1990*	*93*	*66*	*27*	*76*
7	1991	15	10	5	
8	1992	17	13	4	
9	1993	15	14	1	
10	1994	15	15	0	
Subtotal (7–10)	*1991–1994*	*62*	*52*	*10*	
Subtotal (6–10)	*1990–1994*	*78*	*48*	*13*	
Total 1–10	*1985–1994*	*155*	*118*	*37*	

Research Questions

Four sets of outcome questions were the focus of this study, addressing employment, educational, self-sufficiency, and criminality outcomes. In addition, available data allowed for an examination of attrition and a study of the youth-counselor relationship. Following are the specific research questions.

What was the attrition rate, and who dropped out of WAY Scholarship?

♦ What was the attrition rate from the program?

♦ What child and family background characteristics were associated with youth dropping out of the WAY Scholarship program (receiving less than 2.5 years of the 5-year program)?

Did WAY Scholarship youth gain employment experiences and savings?

♦ During their involvement in the WAY Scholarship program, what kinds of employment experiences did youth obtain?

♦ By the end of the program, did scholars have savings from their employment?

♦ As young adults, were the WAY scholars employed?

Did WAY scholars achieve educational success?

♦ Did the WAY scholars have higher educational attainment rates than the comparison youth at the end of the program?

♦ By the end of the program, were the WAY scholars educational achievers?

♦ Did educational achievement rates improve from the end of the program to age 21?

♦ By age 21, did educational achievement rates of the WAY scholars compare favorably to national rates?

Did WAY scholars prepare for self-sufficiency?

♦ By the end of the program, were WAY scholars on a self-sufficiency trajectory either by being in school or employed?

- Was residence following discharge or at the end of the program related to being on a self-sufficiency trajectory?

Did WAY scholars avoid criminality?

- As young adults (22 to 32 years of age), did the WAY scholars have lower criminality rates than the comparison youth?

- Did criminality rates of the WAY scholars compare favorably to national rates?

How did youth feel about their WAY counselors, and was "mentoring" associated with positive outcomes?

- Did WAY scholars experience their counselors as helpful mentors?

- Was the match between counselors and youth or the stability of the relationship associated with positive outcomes?

Sources of Data

Data were collected from seven primary sources: (1) agency records, (2) counselor bimonthly report forms, (3) semistructured interviews with participants as adults, (4) Internet data sets accessible to the public, (5) exit interviews with youth at the end of the five-year program, (6) staff updates, and (7) information obtained from a private detective.

Agency Records

For approximately 80% of the youth in the study, an agency record was available, providing varying amounts of information about their lives up to the time of entry into CV. Most records were available on CV's campus; some that were not on hand (lost to the fire) were obtained from copies held at the offices of the Administration for Children's Services in New York City. Trained researchers coded data from these records for the purposes of sample description and group comparisons. These data were available on WAY Scholarship cohorts 1 to 10 and on the comparison group cohorts 1 to 6.

Bimonthly WAY Scholarship Counselor Report Forms

WAY Scholarship counselor report forms were completed for all scholars approximately every other month. These bimonthly forms contained information regarding the youth's progress toward his education and employment goals. From these forms, all employment and some education data were obtained. Yet, these forms were only available for WAY Scholarship cohorts 6 to 10. Bimonthly reports for cohorts 1 to 5 were not available because the reporting mechanisms during the early years of the program were not comparable to those instituted in subsequent years. Some early bimonthly report forms were also lost in the fire. Thus, variables derived from this source were only available for these 5 cohorts.

Semistructured Interviews

A third source of data was face-to-face semistructured interviews that were conducted with 39 WAY scholars from cohorts 1 to 6 in 1997. Researchers paid youth $50 to participate in an interview about their lives since the time of discharge from CV. Verbatim transcripts of these interviews served as the source of data regarding adult employment, adult educational status, and youth perceptions of the counselors. Variables derived from the interviews were available only for this subset of 39 youths, all of whom were between the ages of 21 and 30 and all of whom had participated in WAY Scholarship for at least 2.5 years.

Public Records Via the Internet

The New York State Department of Corrections (DOCS) website provided data regarding adult criminality of the youth in the study. The website was searched in August 1999 when the former participants were between 22 and 32 years of age. These data were available for WAY Scholarship cohorts 1 to 6 and the comparison cohorts 1 to 6. Although the website could have been searched for WAY Scholarship cohorts 7 to 10, these youth were not old enough for a meaningful assessment of adult criminality.

Exit Interviews

Some youths participated in exit interviews at the time they were completing the 5-year program. Although not every youth completed these interviews and the forms themselves changed over time, they were a useful way to confirm or clarify existing data.

Staff Updates

When youth could not be located for interviews, CV or WAY Scholarship program staff were sometimes able to provide updated information on their whereabouts. In some cases, a staff member was familiar with the status of a youth regarding a particular outcome (e.g., high school graduation, incarceration).

Private Detective

A private detective was hired to find youths who could not otherwise be found. When the detective located past participants, he would interview them to obtain key information missing from the database.

Measures and Data Collection Procedures

Demographics and Family Background
Characteristics Prior to Program Participation

In order to describe the sample of WAY Scholarship youth and in order to compare them with the comparison group, it was necessary to obtain detailed information regarding the sociodemographic characteristics of all youths in the study. Each youth's agency record was coded by trained researchers for demographic information. Fifty-one (51) variables were initially of interest. The records contained consistent information relevant to 27 variables sufficient for data analyses. The 24 variables with insufficient information in the records pertained primarily to the parents, including employment and educational status, prior incarcerations and hospitalizations, and substance abuse problems. Thus, 27 variables obtained from agency records were available for each youth in WAY Scholarship cohorts 1 to 10 and from the comparison group cohorts 1 to 6. The 27 variables are discussed below, and they fall into two categories: (1) demographic and placement history and (2) youth behavior problems.

- ◆ *Demographics and Placement History*—include age at CV placement, age at WAY Scholarship entry, years at CV after enrollment into WAY Scholarship, race, whether a youth was in foster care prior to admission to CV, with whom a youth was living prior to admission, discharge destination after leaving CV, full scale IQ at time of entry to CV, history of being physically abused, history of being sexually abused, history of being neglected, and number of types of abuse experienced.

- ◆ *Youth Behavior Problems*—include history of using illegal substances or alcohol, running away, attempting suicide or ideation, fire setting, truancy, suspension or expulsion from school, cruelty to animals, robbery, violent or aggressive behavior without a weapon, violent or aggressive behavior with a weapon, theft, destruction of property, disorderly conduct, sexual offenses, and total number of documented problems among these 14.

Employment Outcomes

Employment During Program Participation (WAY Scholarship cohorts 6 to 10)

From the counselor bimonthly report forms five employment variables were constructed: (1) number of jobs held, (2) length of jobs, (3) proportion of jobs held on campus (versus in the community), (4) proportion of time in WAY Scholarship that youth held a job, and (5) reasons for leaving jobs.

Employment as Young Adults (WAY Scholarship cohorts 1 to 6 who were interviewed as adults)

From the semistructured interviews with 39 youths from cohorts 1 to 6, we were able to determine employment status as of 1997 when the young men were between 21 and 30 years of age. These data were coded unemployed (0) or employed (1). Annual salaries were calculated based on information provided in the interview.

Educational Outcomes

Educational Status at End of Program (WAY Scholarship cohorts 1 to 10 who participated for at least 2.5 years and comparison youth cohorts 1 to 6 who did not drop out of the comparison group)

Information was obtained from bimonthly report forms, from program and agency staff familiar with the youth, and from the private detective. This variable was coded as dropped out of high school/GED program, currently still in high school/GED program, earned a GED, graduated from high school, was in college but dropped out prior to graduation, or currently in college. Educational attainment data at the end of the program were not available for most youth who dropped out of either WAY Scholarship or out of the comparison group. Thus, analyses of this outcome focused on the 76% of the WAY scholars who participated for at least 2.5 years in the program.

For the purposes of analyses, this variable was recoded as educational achiever (score of 1, in school, graduated from high school, or achieved GED degree) or nonachiever (score of 0, dropped out of school prior to completion of high school degree or GED). The rationale for including GED recipients as comparable to high school graduates is based on the fact that 92% of colleges accept GED graduates for admission and 96% of employers accept the GED as the equivalent of a high school diploma (Russell 1989).[1]

---

1. Male GED recipients tend to earn more than those who drop out of high school and never earn a high school degree or equivalency diploma (Murnane et al. 1995).

Educational Attainment at Age 21 (WAY Scholarship cohorts 1 to 6)

From 39 semistructured interviews and researchers' discussions with staff, we were able to determine the educational level attained by the age of 21 for WAY youth who participated in at least 2.5 years of the program. These data were not available for the comparison group. In some cases these data were self-reported; in other instances (e.g., college attendance) the WAY counselors had firsthand knowledge of educational attainment. In cases where both youth reports and counselor reports were available, these data were found to be consistent. Although not ideal, use of self-report data to assess level of educational attainment was not unique to this study. In fact, the Census Bureau relies on self-report data for calculating national estimates (U.S. Census Bureau 1992).

Educational attainment was coded as dropped out of high school, currently in GED program, earned GED, graduated from high school, attended some college but dropped out before graduating, currently in college, or graduated from college. This variable was recoded as achiever (score of 1, in school, graduated from high school, earned GED, some postsecondary education) or nonachiever (score 0, dropped out of high school before completion of degree or GED).

Self-Sufficiency Outcomes

Self-Sufficiency at End of the Program (WAY Scholarship cohorts 1 to 10 who participated in at least 2.5 years of WAY)

Self-sufficiency data were coded from counselor bimonthly reports, as well as other data sources, and were available for WAY Scholarship youths in cohorts 1 to 10 who participated in at least 2.5 years of the program. Self-sufficiency trajectory was conceptualized as either being employed or achieving educational success by the end of the program and was coded 0 (not in school and not employed) or 1 (in school/graduated from school and/or employed). A more conservative way to measure self-sufficiency was also examined, in which youth had to be in school or employed in order to be coded as self-sufficient. Thus, youth who had completed school but were not currently employed were coded as not being on a self-sufficiency trajectory.

Criminality Outcomes

Criminality at Age 21 (WAY Scholarship and Comparison cohorts 1 to 6)

The Internet website for the New York State DOC was searched (at <www.docs.state.ny.us>) for every youth in the first six cohorts. This website contains a comprehensive listing (dating from the early 1970s) of all persons convicted of a crime who have served jail time in New York State prisons. The search was conducted in August 1999, using name, date of birth, and race as identifiers. This procedure produced information on the date of the sentence, the nature of the crime, the severity of the crime according to DOCS standards, and the length of the jail sentence. Age 21 was selected as the cut-off to control for crimes committed prior to the end of the program. The youth were between 22 and 32 years of age at the time the criminal background search was conducted. The early to middle 20's are generally considered the peak ages for commission of crimes (Evans 1997).

The New York State DOCS database does not include inmates in federal prisons. It also does not include arrests or incarcerations in another state, but most scholarship and comparison group youth resided in the New York City metropolitan area following discharge from CV. Thus, we felt that we would be measuring most incarcerations. The DOCS database also did not include those in New York City or county jails. Yet, because anyone sentenced to terms longer than 1 year are sent to state prisons, the data obtained reflected youth convicted of serious crimes. From this data, four variables were created: whether a crime was committed (0=no crime, 1=at least one crime), length of sentence (in years), type of crime (economic versus violent), and severity of crime (coded on a 5-point scale created by DOCS in which 1 reflects the most severe crimes and 5 reflects the least severe crimes).

Counselor-Youth Relationship Variables

Youth Perception of Counselors (WAY Scholarship cohorts 1 to 6)

From the interviews with 39 WAY scholars cohorts 1 to 6, information was obtained about perceptions of their relationships with WAY counselors. These data were available for the 39 cohorts 1 to 6 youth who were interviewed, all of whom participated in WAY Scholarship for at least 2.5 years.

Match Between Counselor and Youth (WAY Scholarship cohorts 6 to 10)

From the counselor bimonthly report forms, we were able to determine gender and ethnicity matches between youth and their counselors. These data were available for WAY Scholarship youth cohorts 6 to 10. Matches were coded 1 for exact ethnic matches (e.g., white youth with white counselor, black youth with black counselor, and Latino youth with Latino counselor). Nonmatches were coded 0 (e.g., a white youth with a black counselor, a Latino youth with a white counselor). This variable was coded as a continuous variable representing the percentage of months in the program that a youth had a counselor who matched his ethnicity.

Gender matches were coded either 1 (male youth with male counselor) or 0 (male youth with female counselor). For purposes of description, this variable was first treated as a continuous variable, representing the percentage of months the youth was in the program that a youth had a counselor who matched his gender. Because of skewness, this variable was converted into a dichotomous variable (0=never had a female counselor, 1=had a female counselor at some point) for the sake of examining association between gender match and outcomes.

Stability in Counselor Relationship (WAY Scholarship cohorts 6 to 10)

From the bimonthly report forms, we were able to code two aspects of stability of the youth-counselor relationship, the longest time period (in months) that each youth was with the same counselor, and the number of times a youth switched from one counselor to another.

The Study Participants

The Selection Process

WAY Scholarship Cohorts 1 to 6
The process of selecting youth into the WAY Scholarship program was somewhat different between cohorts 1 to 6 and cohorts 7 to 10. For cohorts 1 to 6, the selection process included the creation of the comparison group, whereas for cohorts 7 to 10 no comparison group was created.

During the first 5 years of the program, the policy was to recruit from the RTC, although some exceptions were made to include agency group home or foster home youth (8 youth from group homes and 1 from a foster home in cohorts 1 to 5, 9 of 77, 12%). In cohort 6 and thereafter, the policy changed to allow more group home and foster home youth in the program. For example, 6 of 16 youth in cohort 6 (38%) were recruited from a group home. It is important to note that most youth recruited from the group homes had previous stays at CV's RTC and, therefore, had met the criteria for the highest level of care and had participated in the WAY Works program.

The first step in the selection of WAY scholars was to identify the pool of eligible applicants. A list was created by the research department of youth who met the following criteria: (1) were at least 13 years of age, (2) had at least a third-grade reading level, and

(3) had some experience in WAY Works.[2] Candidates who met these criteria were screened further with a set of evaluation tools created by research and program staff to gather information about the youth from social workers, teachers, recreation coordinators, childcare cottage staff, unit directors, and WAY Works supervisors. Staff rated the youth on maturity, ability to handle supervision, progress in treatment, attitudes, and work habits. From these rating scales youth received a total score indicating their strengths and weaknesses.

The 15 candidates with the highest scores who were expected to be on campus at least another 6 months were interviewed for the WAY Scholarship program. The rationale for the 6-month cut off was based on the belief that youth would need at least 6 months of participation in WAY Scholarship while on campus to establish an attachment to the program and to allow youth and their counselors to develop a relationship. It was felt that youth might not sustain their involvement in the program if they were discharged too soon after enrollment.

Because each year there were usually only 15 to 20 youth who met the criteria and were expected to be on campus for at least another 6 months, the purpose of the selection process was to communicate a sense of achievement and honor rather than to select the youth most likely to suceed in the program. It is important to bear in mind that all youth selected for WAY Scholarship were at high risk for negative outcomes due to the many risk factors present in their lives (e.g., minority status, requiring special education, experiencing abuse or neglect, exhibiting behavior problems).

Once youth were selected into the program, social workers contacted each youth's parents or guardians in order to enroll the youth into the WAY Scholarship program. A standard script was used in these meetings to assure a degree of uniformity. Special effort was made to contact hard-to-reach parents. In some cases, it took several months to arrange meetings. Parents and guardians were asked to attend a meeting with their child, his social worker, and a researcher to discuss project requirements and to answer questions. Both parents and applicants signed an informed consent and a letter of agreement or contract detailing the terms of the program requirements. Terms of the contract included a commitment to work, save, attend workshops, stay in school, and seek tutoring if needed. Spanish versions of all program documents and a translator were available. All parents were given a booklet describing the program and were told that

---

2. WAY Works consisted of employment experiences and work ethics workshops that youth participated in prior to enrollment in WAY Scholarship.

they could call at any time if questions or concerns arose. After the interview process, some youngsters declined to participate (though rarely). In such instances, the next candidate on the list was approached. In this manner, the 93 youth in cohorts 1 to 6 were selected into the WAY Scholarship program.

WAY Scholarship Cohorts 7 to 10

Cohorts 7 to 10 were selected based on the same eligibility requirements as cohorts 1 to 6. That is, they had to be at least 13 years of age, to have at least a 3rd-grade reading level, and to have participated in WAY Works employment and workshops. Yet, the system of rating the youth was eliminated. Potential candidates were identified based on the initial selection criteria and then invited into the program. Youth in cohorts 7 to 10—like those in cohorts 1 to 6—had to sign a contract in order to participate in WAY Scholarship.

For all 10 cohorts, youths were selected by December and formally began the program early the following year after the contract was finalized. Every spring an awards dinner was held to induct the new class of WAY scholars into the program and to recognize the achievements of the current WAY participants.

Comparison Group Cohorts 1 to 6

The process of identifying youths for the comparison group was simultaneous to the selection of youths into the WAY Scholarship program for cohorts 1 to 6. As with the Scholarship group, participation was voluntary, parental approval was necessary, and a decision not to participate would in no way affect discharge planning or services received.

The goal of selecting youths for the comparison group was to identify youths similar to the WAY Scholarship youths. The initial list used to identify WAY scholars also served as the basis for inviting youths into the comparison group. The one difference was that youths selected for the comparison group were scheduled to be discharged from the RTC too soon to be eligible for WAY Scholarship.

Youth not eligible for the WAY Scholarship program because of an imminent discharge were invited to participate in the comparison group. It was explained to youth that inclusion in the comparison group entailed receiving a quarterly newsletter containing helpful information about getting and keeping a job in the community, and having access by phone to a member of CV's staff for advice about work and school-related concerns. In addition, they would be paid to participate in semiannual interviews about their experiences following discharge from CV.[3]

Both Scholarship and comparison groups received a letter informing them that they had been selected because their treatment team considered them to have excellent potential to do well at school and work. Services to both groups were provided to participants for up to 5 years.

A total of 155 youth were enrolled into the WAY Scholarship program in cohorts 1 to 10 (93 in cohorts 1 to 6, and 62 in cohorts 7 to 10), and 76 youth were enrolled into the comparison group cohorts 1 to 6 (Table 1).

Comparability of Youth Selected into WAY Scholarship and Comparison Groups

It was important to determine whether the selection process just described was effective in creating two comparable groups of youth (WAY and comparison). The goal of this process was to have two groups who differed only in whether they participated in the WAY Scholarship program. The one planned difference between the groups was discharge date, with comparison youth expected to leave campus within six months of enrollment and WAY Scholarship youth expected to remain on campus at least six months.

The possibility arose that youth with differing discharge dates might be different in other ways as well. For example, youth who were the same age as the WAY scholars (about 14 years of age at selection) with earlier discharge dates might have come from less troubled families, because having a family deemed by the agency as ready to receive the youth is a major determinant of having a discharge date. Thus, the comparison group might have been comprised of youth with families that required less assistance from the child welfare system than the WAY Scholarship youth. Similarly, the youth themselves must have been perceived as ready to return home sooner than the WAY scholars. Again, it is plausible that the comparison group youth were less troubled than the WAY Scholarship youth in ways that would have led them to have earlier discharge

---

3. The services they received were similar to those now referred to as "Independent Living Skills" (ILS) services, which are provided to youth upon discharge from care, even though WAY was initiated before the ILS legislation and related regulations went into effect.

dates. Both of these explanations of possible differences between the two groups would mean that the comparison group was comprised of youth who were higher functioning to begin with and would, therefore, be expected to have better outcomes, in the absence of program effects. Thus, the study represented a conservative test of the hypothesis that the WAY Scholarship youth would have better outcomes.

Another difference (albeit unplanned) between the groups was that not one youth in the comparison group was recruited from a group home or foster home, while 15 (16%) of WAY Scholarship youth in cohorts 1 to 6 were recruited from a group home or, in one instance, a foster home. Because all but two of the youth recruited into WAY Scholarship from a group home had earlier resided on the campus of the RTC, they met the criteria for the highest level of care. In fact, it is possible that the group home youth were more disadvantaged than the youth recruited into the program from the RTC (including the comparison group) because they did not have a family able to accept them. However, small sample sizes precluded comparisons of youth recruited into WAY Scholarship from a group home and from the RTC campus.

A series of group comparison analyses was conducted to determine whether there were statistically significant differences between the WAY Scholarship cohorts 1 to 6 (93 boys) and comparison group cohorts 1 to 6 (76 boys) at the time they entered CV. The 27 variables described in this chapter were examined. Data on most variables were available on 83% of the WAY Scholarship youth and 63% of the 76 comparison youth. Table 2 presents the frequency distributions of each variable by group and the results of the significance tests.

In most respects, the selection process was successful at creating two comparable groups of youth. The groups were similar in age, race, length of time in care, IQ, and 14 behavior problems. However, 3 of the 27 variables (11%) were statistically significant, more than the number expected by chance alone. WAY Scholarship youth were more likely to have had prior foster care placements, more likely to have been neglected, and experienced more types of abuse. These differences suggest that the comparison group was at an advantage compared to the WAY group, an advantage that allowed them to have an earlier discharge from the RTC. It is important to consider these differences with caution due to the high percentage of missing data, especially in the comparison group. Yet, we believe that the incidence of missing data is random and, therefore, would probably not affect the analyses. Because the comparison youth appear to be at an advantage compared to WAY Scholarship youth, the analyses of group differences on outcomes represent a conservative test of the study hypotheses.

Who were the WAY Scholarship Youth?

One hundred and fifty-five (155) youth were selected into the WAY Scholarship program cohorts 1 to 10. They were enrolled between January 1985 and January 1994. Table 3 presents child and family background characteristics of these youngsters at the time of arrival at CV. For most of the 27 variables, data were available on at least 129 of 155 (83%) youth at the time the retrospective search was conducted.

As can be seen in the table, the youth enrolled in WAY Scholarship cohorts 1 through 10 were of minority racial and ethnic status (61.7% black, 28.2% Latino, and 10.1% white). The majority (73.5%) had prior out-of-home placements in the foster care system before CV, although almost half (47.5%) were living with one or both parents immediately prior to arrival at CV. About 31% were living with a relative, friend, or other person; and 22% came to CV directly from an institutional setting such as another agency's group home, another RTC, or a psychiatric hospital.

A look at formal test scores revealed that the average full scale IQ prior to entry to CV was 91, in the low-average range of intelligence. However, there was substantial variation among WAY scholars in IQ scores, with a low of 61 and a high of 133 (Mean=91, Standard Deviation [SD]=13.00). Most scholars had histories of being maltreated. Many were physically abused (66.2%) or neglected by parents or other primary caretakers (75.2%). Nine percent had known histories of being sexually abused.[4]

A wide variety of problem behaviors were exhibited by these youth prior to placement at CV. Violent or aggressive behavior characterized most youth (73.6%). Also common were such behaviors as running away (41.1%); attempting suicide or suicidal ideation (36.4%); and theft (36.4%), most commonly involving money or objects in the home. Also common was truancy (32.6%) and being suspended or expelled from school (25.6%). Less common problem behaviors were destruction of property, fire play, sexual offenses, violent behavior using a weapon, the use of illegal substances or alcohol, robbery, and disorderly conduct. Of the 14 problem behaviors examined, scholars on average were found to have been involved in about 3, although the range was 0 to 8 (Mean=3.18, SD=1.75).

---

4. This number is likely to be an underestimation because of underreporting.

Table 2: Comparison of Background Characteristics at Time of Placement at CV for WAY and Comparison Groups (Cohorts 1 to 6)

Background Characteristics	WAY (Full sample = 93)		Comparison (Full sample = 76)		P
Demographics and Placement History	mean	*Valid N*	mean	*Valid N*	
Age at CV Placement*	12.2	71	11.8	60	–
Age at WAY Entry	14.2	93	14.2	76	–
Years at CV after WAY Entry*	1.3	61	.9	51	–
IQ (Full Scale)	90.4	78	89.3	50	–
Race	%	88	%	73	–
Black	62.5%		63.0%		–
Latino	22.7%		20.5%		–
White	14.8%		16.4%		–
Youth in Foster Care prior to CV	73.3%	75	48.8%	43	.01
Who Youth Lived with Prior to CV		77		50	–
Single Parent	51.9%		44.0%		–
Both Parents	6.5%		8.0%		–
Other Family (Relatives, Friends)	28.6%		30.0%		–
Agency	13.0%		18.0%		–
Discharge Destination*		74		43	–
Family Environment	48.6%		66.7%		–
Structured Group Setting	51.4%		33.3%		–
% Physically Abused	64.9%	77	46.8%	47	–
% Neglected/Abandoned	70.1%	77	42.6%	47	.00
% Sexually Abused	5.2%	77	6.4%	47	–
	mean		mean		
Mean Number of Types of Abuse	1.4	77	1.0	47	.00
History of Behavior Problems	%	77	%	48	p
Violence/Aggression	71.4%		81.3%		–
Theft	35.1%		39.6%		–
Suicidal Ideation/Acts	35.1%		27.1%		–
Truancy from School	35.1%		25.0%		–
Running Away	29.9%		27.1%		–
School Expulsion/ Suspension	26.0%		18.8%		–
Destroying Property	23.4%		18.8%		–
Fire Play	15.6%		29.2%		–
Sexual Offense	11.7%		8.3%		–
Using a Weapon	11.7%		10.4%		–
Using Illegal Drugs/Alcohol	6.5%		2.1%		–
Disorderly Conduct	6.5%		0.0%		–
Cruelty to Animals	5.2%		4.2%		–
Robbery	2.6%		2.1%		–
Mean Number of Behavior Problems	3.0		2.9		–

* Excludes 14 youth selected into WAY Scholarship from group homes and 1 from a foster home.

Table 3: Background Characteristics of WAY Scholars (Cohorts 1 to 10)

Background Characteristics		(Full sample = 155 Scholars)	
Demographics and Placement History	Mean		Valid N
Age at CV Placement*	12.1		122
Age at WAY Entry	14.2		155
Years at CV after WAY Entry*	1.3		111
IQ (Full Scale)	91.1		126
Race	n	Valid %	149
African American	92	61.7%	
Hispanic	42	28.2%	
White	15	10.1%	
Youth in Foster Care Prior to CV	98	73.5%	132
Who Youth Lived with Prior to CV			131
Single Parent	55	42.0%	
Both Parents	7	5.3%	
Other Family (Relatives, Friends)	40	30.5%	
Agency	29	22.1%	
Discharge Destination*			125
Family Environment	54	43.2%	
Structured Group Setting	71	56.8%	
% Physically Abused	88	66.2%	133
% Neglected/Abandoned	100	75.2%	133
% Sexually Abused	12	9.2%	131
	mean		
Mean Number of Types of Abuse	1.5		132
History of Behavior Problems	n	Valid %	129
Violence/Aggression	95	73.6%	
Running Away	53	41.1%	
Suicidal Ideation/Acts	47	36.4%	
Theft	47	36.4%	
Truancy from School	42	32.6%	
School Expulsion/ Suspension	33	25.6%	
Destroying Property	27	20.9%	
Fire Play	22	17.1%	
Using a Weapon	17	13.2%	
Sexual Offense	16	12.4%	
Using Illegal Drugs/Alcohol	8	6.2%	
Disorderly Conduct	5	3.9%	
Cruelty to Animals	4	3.1%	
Robbery	4	3.1%	
Mean Number of Behavior Problems	3.2		129

* Excludes 20 youth selected into WAY Scholarship from group homes
and 6 from foster homes.

In summary, the background characteristics of WAY scholars seemed to mirror the larger population of youngsters at CV. Scholars were likely to be from ethnic minority backgrounds and to have had prior placements within the foster care system. Although the details varied, almost all had histories of being abused and of exhibiting problem behaviors. The overall pattern that emerged is one of a population of youth with characteristics and histories that placed them at risk for educational failure, for unemployment or underemployment, and for criminality. Once in care at CV, all youth underwent educational testing and placement. Nearly all youth were classified as requiring special education and being seriously emotionally disturbed. Although data for the sample were not available, most youth at CV were several years behind academically.

Home Communities

In addition to individual and family characteristics, we also examined the neighborhoods from which the study youth came in order to better understand the community factors that might have shaped their lives. Using geographically based data and visual maps of the communities of origin, three sociodemographic measures representing the three major outcomes of interest in this study were examined: high school graduation rates, employment rates, and reported violent crime rates.

The referral addresses (often mother's address) where youth lived prior to admission to CV were identified for all but 14 scholars. In addition, 21 youth had addresses that were outside of New York City and were, therefore, omitted from this analysis. The remaining 120 valid New York City addresses were from Brooklyn (46), the Bronx (31), Manhattan (27), Queens (12), and Staten Island (4).

Figure 2 shows the New York City referral addresses where youth lived prior to admission to CV.[5] As can be seen, although youth lived throughout New York City, they tended to cluster in specific neighborhoods. Half of the youth came from just 10 of the city's 59 Community Districts, in north-central Brooklyn, northern Manhattan, and the South Bronx. Five of these Community Districts are among those identified as the communities in New York City least conducive to children's well-being (Citizens' Committee for the Children of New York 1997).

---

5. These maps were created using MapInfo desktop mapping Geographic Information Systems software. The addresses were matched ("geocoded") to their location based on street addresses using the LION street file obtained from the New York City Department of City Planning.

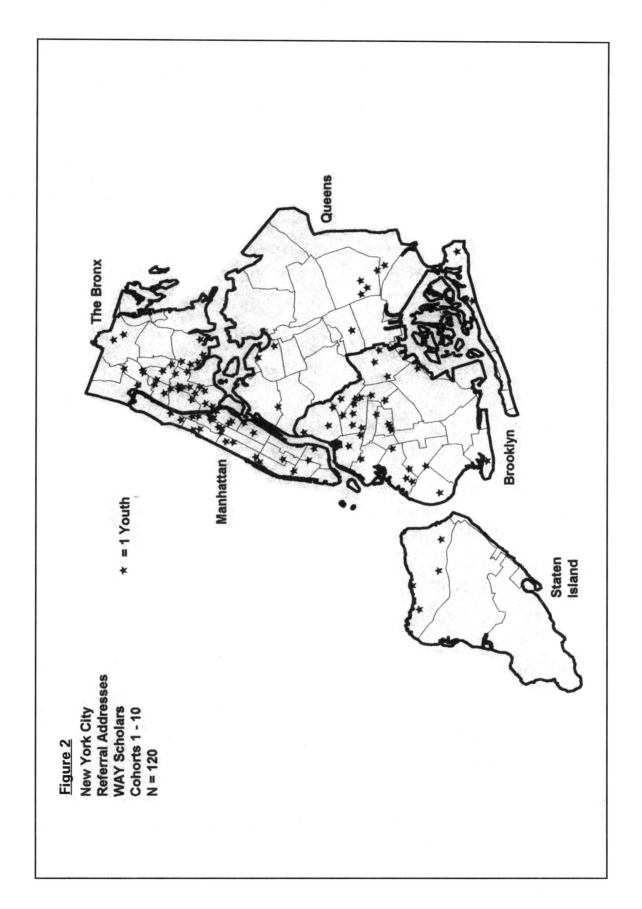

Figure 2
New York City
Referral Addresses
WAY Scholars
Cohorts 1 - 10
N = 120

★ = 1 Youth

The Bronx

Queens

Manhattan

Brooklyn

Staten
Island

Figure 3 illustrates how level of education (the percent of the population over age 25 with a high school degree or GED) varies across the city, according to the 1990 U.S. Census.[6] As can be seen, in one-fifth of the census tracts barely half of the population over the age of 25 had received high school or equivalency diplomas. Most important, it can be seen that the neighborhoods in which the WAY youth lived (and in which their families continued to live while they were in care at CV) had some of the city's lowest educational achievement rates.

Figure 4 illustrates New York City levels of employment, as measured by the percentage of males 16 and over who worked during 1989. The largest areas of high unemployment (north-central Brooklyn, northern Manhattan, and south Bronx) are areas in which many of the study youth lived. Thus, the WAY Scholarship youths living in these neighborhoods were less likely to encounter working adults than youths living in areas with higher employment rates.

Figure 5 shows the percentage of the population under 18 living in poverty, according to the 1990 U.S. Census. It can again be seen that some neighborhoods fare better than others, with the poorer areas being northern Manhattan and portions of Brooklyn. It is clear that those enrolled in WAY Scholarship tended to come from neighborhoods where residents had below average levels of education, high unemployment rates, and where many youth lived in poverty.

Figure 6 shows the number of reported violent felonies in 1994 by community district. The high crime areas include Bedford-Stuyvesant, east New York, Brownsville in Brooklyn, Jamaica in Queens, central Harlem and east Harlem in Manhattan, and Unionport/Soundview in the Bronx.[7] It can be seen that many of the WAY scholars grew up in environments where they were likely to be exposed to high levels of violence.

---

6. The unit of analysis for Figures 3 to 6 is the census tract, considered by many researchers to be a good proxy for a neighborhood because the units are small (with only a few thousand residents on average) and the boundaries are drawn based on social and demographic factors as well as geographic features such as streets and rivers (Masey & Denton 1993). There were 2,216 census tracts in New York City according to the 1990 U.S. Census.
7. This crime data and the community profiles that follow are reported in Keeping Track of New York City's Children (The Citizens' Committee for the Children of New York 1997).7. This crime data and the community profiles that follow are reported in Keeping Track of New York City's Children (The Citizens' Committee for the Children of New York 1997).

These geographic patterns suggest that those living in low-income neighborhoods are actually the most likely to be victimized by crime. Indeed, data from the National Crime Victimization Survey indicate that as household income levels decrease, rates of violent crime and burglary increase (Ringel 1997).

In all, Figures 2 to 6 reveal that the WAY Scholarship youth tended to come from dangerous, low-income neighborhoods with low educational attainment rates and many unemployed adults. Many of these neighborhoods are composed of predominantly minority residents. The fact that New York City, like many urban areas, contains such high concentrations of black families in relatively small areas has led two prominent sociologists to conclude that New York qualifies as a "hypersegregated" city (Massey & Denton 1993). According to the 1990 U.S. Census, 68% of the entire population living in New York City over age 25 had at least a high school or equivalency diploma, 72% of the males 16 or older worked during 1989, and 30% of the youth under 18 lived in poverty. For the population living in the census tracts where at least one WAY youth lived prior to arrival at CV, these averages were much different. Only 58% of those 25 and over had a high school education, just 44% of the males 16 and over were employed, and 45% of the youth under 18 lived in poverty.

A closer examination of the two Community Districts with the highest concentrations of WAY Scholarship enrollees, Bedford-Stuyvesant in Brooklyn and Morrisania in the Bronx, revealed in more detail the kinds of communities in which many of these youth were raised. Bedford-Stuyvesant (Figure 7), where 9 of the 120 youth were from, is a largely black area in Brooklyn. According to the Citizens' Committee for the Children of New York (1997), its population in 1990 was 138,696. Over 69% of the 2,813 children born in 1994 were born into poverty. Over half of the households had annual incomes in 1993 under $10,000. Figure 7 shows the location in Brooklyn of the Bedford-Stuyvesant Community District and the youth poverty levels of the census tracts within it.

On the other side of the city in the Bronx is the Community District of Morrisania, where seven WAY Scholarship youths lived (Figure 8). The Citizens' Committee for the Children of New York (1997) describes this as a largely Latino community with a population of 58,345, 41% of whom were under 18 years of age. Seventy-six percent of the youth were born into poverty in 1994. Over half of the households had annual incomes under $10,000. The unemployment rate was over 17%; and, as of 1993, barely 5% of the population owned their own homes.

These seven maps and the sociodemographic data in Table 3 illustrate that, as a group, the WAY Scholarship youth came from poor neighborhoods with many risk factors for negative outcomes (such as low educational success rates, high crime rates, and high unemployment). In order to provide a more detailed picture of the lives of the WAY Scholarship youth, following the maps are in-depth early histories of two youth.

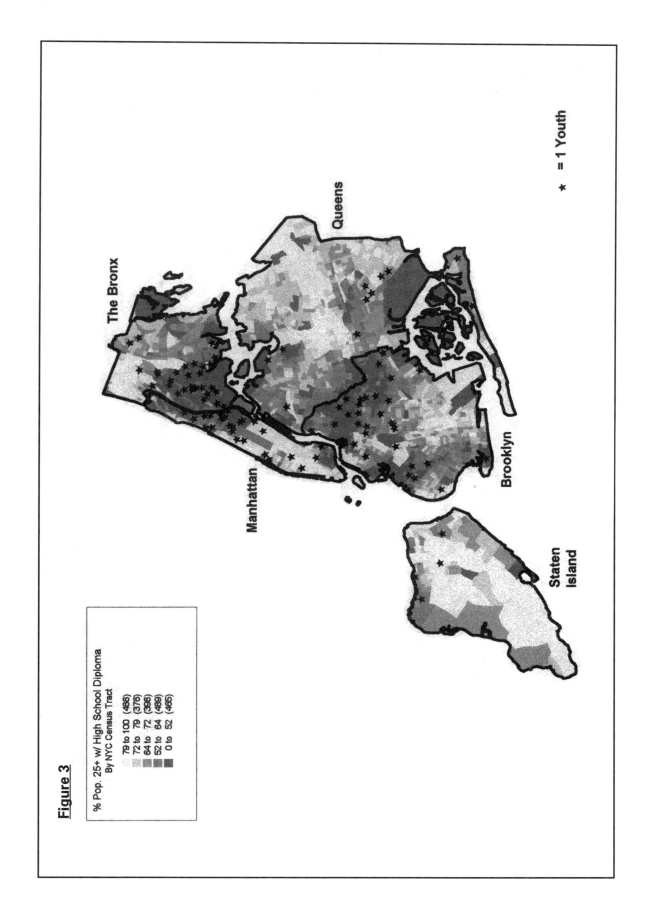

Figure 3

% Pop. 25+ w/ High School Diploma
By NYC Census Tract

79 to 100 (488)
72 to 79 (376)
64 to 72 (398)
52 to 64 (489)
0 to 52 (465)

The Bronx

Manhattan

Queens

Brooklyn

Staten Island

★ = 1 Youth

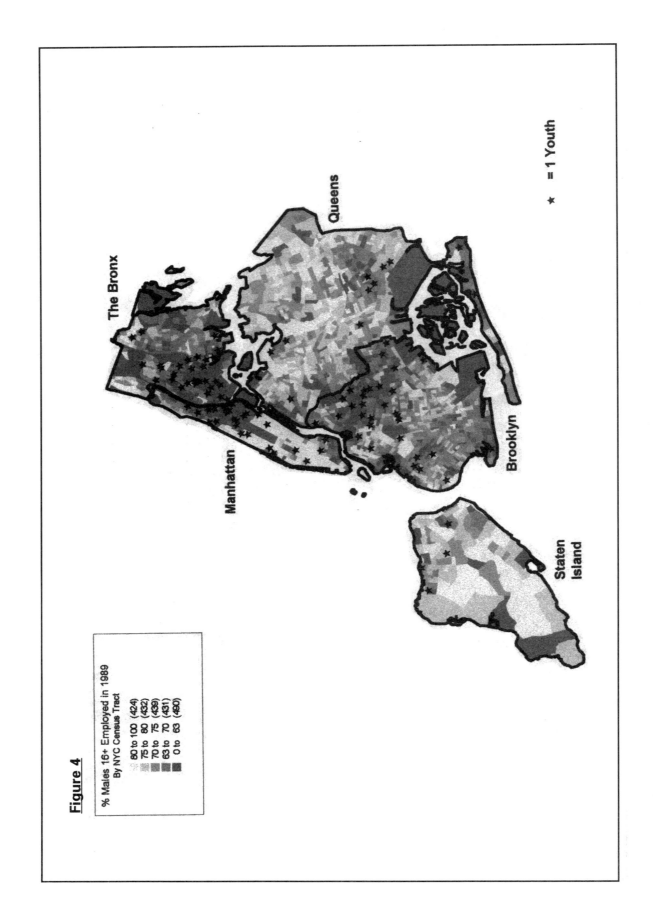

Figure 4

% Males 16+ Employed in 1989
By NYC Census Tract

80 to 100 (424)
75 to 80 (432)
70 to 75 (439)
63 to 70 (431)
0 to 63 (490)

The Bronx

Manhattan

Queens

Brooklyn

Staten Island

★ = 1 Youth

Figure 5

% Youth Under 18 In Poverty
By NYC Census Tract

- 0 to 5 (543)
- 5 to 11 (327)
- 11 to 21 (405)
- 21 to 37 (415)
- 37 to 100 (526)

The Bronx

Manhattan

Queens

Brooklyn

Staten Island

★ = 1 Youth

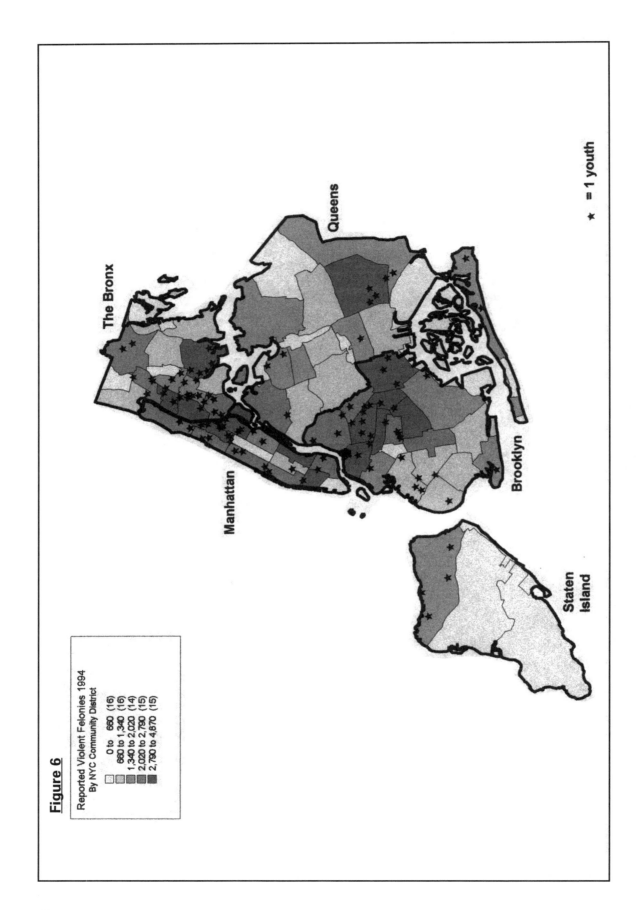

Figure 6

Reported Violent Felonies 1994
By NYC Community District

☐	0 to 660 (16)
☐	660 to 1,340 (16)
☐	1,340 to 2,020 (14)
☐	2,020 to 2,790 (15)
☐	2,790 to 4,870 (15)

The Bronx

Queens

Manhattan

Brooklyn

Staten Island

★ = 1 youth

Figure 7

% Youth Under 18 In Poverty
By NYC Census Tract

☐ 0 to 5 (543)
☐ 5 to 11 (327)
☐ 11 to 21 (405)
☐ 21 to 37 (415)
■ 37 to 100 (526)

Bedford Styvesant, Brooklyn

★ WAY Scholar Referral Address

Community District 3

Figure 8

% Youth Under 18 In Poverty
By NYC Census Tract

0 to 5	(543)
5 to 11	(327)
11 to 21	(405)
21 to 37	(415)
37 to 100	(526)

Morrisania, The Bronx

★ WAY Scholar Referral Address

Community District 3

Youth Biography: Hugo

Prior to being placed in foster care at age 11, Hugo was living with his widowed mother and his older stepsister (with whom he shared a room) in a dangerous, drug-infested neighborhood on Manhattan's Lower East Side. A heavy user of drugs and alcohol, his father died of liver failure at age 27. The family survived on public assistance.

Hugo's parents were raised in violent or rejecting families and were unable to cope effectively as adults. His father had been beaten by both of his parents, and the pattern of violence continued into his adult relationships with women. Hugo's mother had endured severe abuse—including rape—at the hands of Hugo's father. The children often witnessed these scenes of domestic violence. Hugo's mother was rejected very early on by an alcoholic mother; later in life she attempted suicide twice. Unemployed, she sought help through therapy and by taking tranquilizers.

In 1986, 9-year-old Hugo was referred by his school to a Manhattan-based outpatient clinic. The behaviors that led to psychological counseling, and later to his mother's decision to place Hugo in residential treatment, included truancy, fire setting, theft, explosive outbursts, fighting, and threatening to kill his mother. Intake notes from the first contact at the clinic indicated that, "One gets the sense that [Hugo] often feels overwhelmed by his own anger and [is] out of control."

His mother reported that Hugo's behavior had always been worse at home than elsewhere, such as school or recreational activities. Moreover, it had deteriorated markedly following his father's death. The clinic report concluded that, "Without a positive father figure to emulate, Hugo seems intent on emulating his deceased father, who went AWOL from the Marines, dealt drugs, beat Hugo's mother, and died of alcoholism."

In 1987, the family endured a series of crises that became too much for Hugo to bear. His 15-year-old sister tried to commit suicide and was briefly hospitalized. Afterward, she married her teenaged boyfriend, who moved in with the family. Hugo then had to share a bedroom with his mother. Around that time, Hugo's mother suffered a brutal mugging and attack. She, too, was hospitalized and underwent surgery. During her recovery, she put Hugo in the awkward position of assisting with her personal care. According to the family's caseworker, the mother was not only sexually provocative, but was also angry, manipulative, and sometimes sadistic toward her son.

Furthermore, a visit with his paternal grandparents raised the specter of Hugo's father and put the young boy in the middle of an ongoing family battle. His grandmother repeatedly insisted that Hugo's mother was to blame for his father's death. This led to severe conflicts between mother and son that took the form of emotional manipulation as well as outright physical fighting. Psychological reports characterized these scenes as Hugo's mother seeking revenge on her husband through her son, who took on the father's role in escalating tensions. These episodes reached a peak when Hugo went on a rampage, breaking objects in the house and attempting to attack his mother and sister with a knife.

At the end of 1987, Hugo spent 2 months at a diagnostic center, where he received full psychological, psychiatric, and educational evaluations. As noted earlier by his mother, Hugo's behavior had always been more manageable outside of the home; indeed, he adjusted well to this initial placement, where he lived in a cottage, went to school, and participated in recreational and religious activities. Hugo was considered a good candidate for residential treatment. The next year, he made a smooth transition to CV, where he was placed voluntarily by his mother. He took advantage of the enrichment provided on the campus and soon was actively participating in the early stages of the WAY program. Within 16 months, he was chosen to be a WAY scholar and continued with the program after a successful discharge home.

Youth Biography: Andrew

Andrew's is a story of a traumatic early history, a second chance, disappointment, despair, and new beginnings. As recounted to a psychologist when Andrew was 11.5 years old, this child's early history, at first hearing, seemed almost too fantastic to be true. "In speaking to Andrew, one was struck by his ability to express his feelings and [by his] excellent vocabulary. Sadness permeated everything he said..."

Born to a 14-year-old mother, Andrew was given up shortly after birth to live with his maternal grandmother. For 4.5 years, he existed in a state of severe neglect. He was not toilet trained, nor did he speak. Returned to his birth mother, within 6 months he was again given up, and at age 5 he entered the foster care system. He then endured several years during which he was passed from one foster home to another. Describing what he was going through during that period, Andrew explained "I feel like an envelope flying in the air going from house to house. By the time I get to one place the envelope is ripped."

Although he could not recall the exact number of foster homes he was sent to—the total was between 7 and 10—Andrew reported having miserable experiences in each one of them. He recounted being severely beaten, burned, even held under water, among other abuses. As a result, he lived with the scars of these traumas. Externally, he had multiple bruises on his body; internally, he felt unwanted, unloved, and wary of trusting others. At an early age, he was placed in special education for emotional disturbance.

For a time, he did find a stable home environment with a foster family. This older couple, who had already raised children of their own, ultimately adopted Andrew when he was 9 years old. However, within months, the behaviors that had jeopardized his adjustment in the classroom and at previous foster families became too much for his adoptive parents to handle. Andrew was sent to CV the first time shortly before his tenth birthday. There he received the intensive and individualized treatment he desperately needed.

(Andrew's case history, continued)

After 2 years, he returned home on a trial basis, but it was apparent that a final discharge from residential treatment was premature. He was suspended from school and still too much for his adoptive parents to handle. He returned to CV within 3 months. During this period he suffered another severe blow. His adoptive parents refused further contact with Andrew and decided to give up their parental rights. Andrew was rejected by the one set of parents who had tried to give him a long-term home and family.

This second stay at CV proved crucial to Andrew's growth and future. He became a WAY Scholar, and at age 16 he transferred from the RTC to a group home in the community. Remaining a special education student, he adjusted well to his new school and devoted much of his energies to musical and artistic activities. At the same time, he was paired with a volunteer in the community. The relationship he formed with this man would turn out to be one of the most important for Andrew. After several years of getting to know Andrew, sharing the good and bad times, his volunteer legally adopted him. At the age of 20, this WAY Scholar entered a new permanent family.

5

Findings: What was the
Attrition Rate, and Who
Dropped Out of WAY?

What was the attrition rate from the program?

♦ Only 24% of the WAY youth dropped out of the 5-year program (participated for less than 2.5 years).

♦ Program retention rates improved from cohorts 1 to 6 (29% attrition) to cohorts 7 to 10 (16% attrition), a difference that was marginally statistically significant.

Five years was an unheard-of length of expected participation in a program, especially for adolescents. Participation in the WAY Scholarship program was strictly voluntary; staff had no leverage to enforce participation. Therefore, it was of no surprise that not all youth who began WAY Scholarship remained active for 5 years. Thus, we were able to ask about who dropped out of the program and whether dropouts differed in any ways from those who remained involved. For the sake of such analyses, it was decided that youth who participated for less than 2.5 years (half) of the 5-year program would be considered program dropouts. This is an arbitrary cut-off based on discussions between program staff and researchers.

Of the 155 youth enrolled in the WAY Scholarship program across the first 10 cohorts, 37 (24%) left the program before 2.5 years. The dropout rate for cohorts 1 to 6 alone was 29% (27 of 93) and for cohorts 7 to 10 was only 16%. These differences were marginally statistically significant (Chi-square [n=155]=3.4, p < .07). The overall rate of 24% attrition from the 5-year WAY program is relatively low compared to participation rates of other programs. For example, YIEPP (Farkas et al. 1984) demonstrated 66% participation rates, measured by whether youth were working for at least 2 weeks, a considerably lower standard than 2.5 years of participation in WAY. Quantum Opportunities (Hahn 1994) reported a 40% dropout rate for their 4-year program (though what constituted a dropout was unclear); and in YouthBuild (Ferguson & Clay 1996) only 7% of youth remained involved into the 2nd year of the program. Yet, over half of the youth were reported to have left because they obtained full-time employment. It is clear from these examples that each program conceptualizes participation and attrition differently, making it difficult to develop a basis of comparison for the 24% dropout rate of the WAY program.

Which child and family background characteristics were associated with leaving the program before 2.5 years of participation?

♦ Youth who dropped out of WAY Scholarship were older at enrollment into the program, were discharged from CV's campus significantly sooner, and experienced fewer types of abuse.

These 2 groups were compared on the 27 child and family background variables in order to ascertain whether the youth who eventually dropped out of WAY were different in some way from the beginning. Data were available on 98 of the 118 youth who participated for at least 2.5 years (83%) and 31 of the 37 program dropouts (84%), as revealed in Table 4.

Of the 27 variables examined, 3 (11.1%) significantly differed by group. Compared to scholars who remained active, youth who dropped out of WAY were older (Mean=14.1 years, SD =1.2) at enrollment into WAY than youth who remained active for at least 2.5 years (Mean=14.0, SD=1.0) (t [153]=2.2, p < .05). Youth who dropped out (Mean=0.9 years, SD=.7) were discharged from CV's campus sooner than youth who remained active for at least 2.5 years (Mean=1.4, SD=1.3) (t [71.8]=2.8, p < .01). Youth who dropped out (Mean=1.3, SD=.73) experienced fewer types of documented abuse before entry to CV than youth who remained active for at least 2.5 years (Mean=1.6, SD=.73) (t [130]=2.1, p < .05).

Being older at enrollment into WAY, leaving the campus sooner, and experiencing fewer types of abuse at home were all associated with dropping out of the program. The fact that youth who were discharged from campus sooner were less likely to stay involved in WAY Scholarship suggests that youth were more likely to make a commitment to the program when they lived at CV for the initial period of involvement. This finding is

Table 4: Comparison of WAY and WAY Dropouts on Background Characteristics at Time of Placement at CV (Cohorts 1 to 10)

Background Characteristics	WAY (Full sample = 118)		Dropouts (Full sample = 37)		p
Demographics and Placement History	mean	*Valid N*	mean	*Valid N*	
Age at CV Placement*	12.02	95	12.29	27	–
Age at WAY Entry	14.05	118	14.55	35	.05
Years at CV after WAY Entry*	1.41	85	0.86	26	.01
IQ (Full Scale)	90.13	97	94.21	29	–
Race	%	118	%	31	
African American	65.3%		48.4%		–
Hispanic	25.4%		38.7%		–
White	9.3%		12.9%		–
Youth in Foster Care Prior to CV	75.2%	101	67.7%	31	–
Who Youth Lived with Prior to CV		99		32	
Single Parent	39.4%		50.0%		–
Both Parents	5.1%		6.3%		–
Other Family (Relatives, Friends)	32.3%		25.0%		–
Agency	23.2%		18.8%		–
Discharge Destination*		100		25	
Family Environment	42.0%		48.0%		–
Structured Group Setting	58.0%		52.0%		–
% Physically Abused	68.6%	102	58.1%	31	–
% Neglected/Abandoned	78.4%	102	64.5%	31	–
% Sexually Abused	11.0%	100	3.2%	31	–
	mean		mean		
Mean Number of Types of Abuse	1.57	101	1.26	31	.05
History of Behavior Problems	%	98	%	31	p
Violence/Aggression	71.4%		80.6%		–
Running Away	41.8%		35.5%		–
Suicidal Ideation/Acts	37.8%		32.3%		–
Theft	33.7%		45.2%		–
Truancy from School	29.6%		41.9%		–
School Expulsion/ Suspension	23.5%		32.3%		–
Destroying Property	19.4%		25.8%		–
Fire Play	13.3%		29.0%		–
Sexual Offense	13.3%		9.7%		–
Using a Weapon	12.2%		16.1%		–
Using Illegal Drugs/Alcohol	6.1%		6.5%		–
Robbery	4.1%		0.0%		–
Disorderly Conduct	4.1%		3.2%		–
Cruelty to Animals	3.1%		3.2%		–
Mean Number of Behavior Problems	3.06		3.55		–

* Excludes 14 youth selected into WAY Scholarship from group homes and 1 from a foster home.

consistent with the programmatic goal of developing a relationship with youth before they are discharged from CV and return to the community. A final analysis was conducted in order to determine the total amount of variance in dropping out that was accounted for by these three background variables. Results of a multiple logistic regression resulted in a Nagelkerke analogue r square of 18%. Thus, less than 20% of the variance in dropping out can be attributed to these background characteristics. This analysis suggests that factors beyond sociodemographic background variables account for why some youth dropped out of the WAY Scholarship program.

6

Findings: Did WAY Scholarship Youth Gain Employment Experiences and Savings?

Employment findings are reported for 77 of the 78 WAY Scholarship youths in cohorts 6 to 10 (1 youth was missing all employment records). Savings data were available for WAY Scholarship youth cohorts 1 to 10. Some analyses were also conducted on a subset of youth—those who participated for at least 2.5 years of the program (76% of the participants).

During involvement in the WAY Scholarship program, what kinds of employment experiences did the youths obtain?

- ◆ The youth held on average 4.3 jobs while involved in WAY, working on and off campus and in their communities once discharged from care. The youths worked on average 36% of their time in the program.

- ◆ Jobs lasted on average almost 3.5 months (range = under 1 month to 26 months).

- ◆ Over two-thirds of the youth were never fired from a job during their involvement in WAY Scholarship.

The number and type of employment experiences held by the WAY scholars in cohorts 6 to 10 were collected from the bimonthly report forms. From these counselor reports, five variables were created for each scholar: (1) number of jobs held, (2) length of each job, (3) proportion of all jobs held that were located on CV's campus, (4) proportion of the total active time in the program spent working, and (5) reasons jobs ended. We began by looking at the total number of jobs held for each youth.

As can be seen in Table 5, the number of jobs ranged from a minimum of 0 (3 scholars) to a maximum 10 (1 scholar). The mean number of jobs was 4.32. Although some scholars were not active for the entire duration of the program and patterns of involvement were not always consistent over time, these data suggest that scholars averaged almost 1 job per year. The modal number of jobs held was 4; 18 youth (23%) held 4 jobs.

Table 5: Number of Jobs Held by WAY Scholars During the 5-Year Program (Cohorts 6 to 10)

Jobs Held	N	%
0	3	3.9%
1	8	10.4%
2	8	10.4%
3	9	11.7%
4	18	23.4%
5	5	6.5%
6	12	15.6%
7	4	5.2%
8	6	7.8%
9	3	3.9%
10	1	1.3%
TOTAL	**77**	**100%**

Mean = 4.32, SD = 2.43

Most youth worked both on and off campus during their participation in WAY Scholarship. On-campus jobs were held at the WAY Level 3 worksites described in chapter 3 (e.g., Village Store, computer bus). Youths held between 0 and 5 on-campus jobs. These accounted for about one-third of all jobs (30%). Once discharged from the campus of CV, youths varied in their ability to find employment. Some scholars were discharged to communities with limited employment opportunities, especially for minority, low-income teens. Many scholars were under the age of 16 when discharged and needed to obtain working papers in order to be eligible for jobs in their communities. When too young to obtain jobs, youths were encouraged to volunteer and do community service.[1] Despite the challenges faced by the youth in obtaining employment upon discharge, about two-thirds of all WAY Scholarship jobs were held off campus (both in the local community near CV and in the communities to which scholars were discharged).

It is important to bear in mind that employment was but one of two major emphases in the WAY program, with education being the other. It was not expected that youth would be continuously employed for their entire participation in the program. Taking a break from employment to focus on academic pursuits, extracurricular activities, or to attend to pressing family or personal problems was considered part of the journey toward adulthood. Thus, analyses of proportion of time active in the program that each youth worked revealed an average of 36%.

In addition to encouraging youth to seek employment, the WAY Scholarship program philosophy also emphasized keeping jobs. Table 6 presents the frequency distribution of the length of each job. In all, 333 jobs were held by the 77 youths. Start and end dates were available for all but 20 (some jobs continued after the end of the program, and some jobs had missing beginning or end dates). As can be seen, the shortest job was less than 1 month and the longest job was 26 months. The average length of a job was about 3.5 months (Mean=3.45, SD=3.3).

In addition to getting and keeping jobs, youth were also taught how to leave a job. Work ethics workshops were developed to teach youth how to resolve on-the-job conflicts, how to persevere at a job in spite of apparent obstacles, and—when necessary— how to terminate a job in a responsible manner. These workshops were offered to youth in WAY Works and in WAY Scholarship. Throughout the WAY Scholarship program, counselors were to continuously reinforce these skills and attitudes.

Analyses were conducted to examine the reasons youth left the 313 jobs with known start and end dates and for which we could ascertain the reasons for leaving. Possible reasons included job ending (e.g., summer employment), moving, quitting, getting fired, switching jobs, and other (Table 7).

---

1. Unfortunately, these data are not available.

Table 6: Length of Jobs Held by WAY Scholars by End of the 5-Year Program (Cohorts 6 to 10)

Length of Job in Months	N	%
0	1	0.3%
1	111	35.5%
2	45	14.4%
3	55	17.6%
4	22	7.0%
5	25	8.0%
6	15	4.8%
7–12	31	9.9%
13–24	7	2.2%
26	1	0.3%
TOTAL	**313**	**100%**

Mean = 3.45 Months, SD = 3.32

Table 7: Reasons for Leaving Jobs (Cohorts 6 to 10)

Reason	Valid N *	Valid %
Job Ended	79	30.5%
Moved	57	22.0%
Quit	46	17.8%
Fired	35	13.5%
Switched Jobs	33	12.7%
Other	9	3.5%
TOTAL	**259**	**100%**

* Missing data on 47 jobs.

Analyses revealed that almost one-third (n=79, 30.5%) of the jobs were left because the job ended. The next most frequent reason for a youth leaving a job was moving (n=57, 22%), highlighting the transitory nature of these youths' living arrangements (a fact of life for many young adults making the transition out of foster care) and its effect on sustaining employment. Taken together, job ending and moving accounted for over half of all reasons for leaving jobs (n=136, 52.5%). Forty-six jobs (17.8%) ended because youth quit. Examination of counselor reports revealed that some youth quit their jobs for what might be considered good cause, including going back to school, allocating more time to academic pursuits, and wanting to focus more on extracurricular activities. Thirty-three jobs (12.7%) ended when youth switched to a new job, sometimes within the same organization. Nine jobs (3%) ended for unspecified reasons, and only 35 jobs (13.5%) ended in termination. Closer inspection of the 35 jobs that ended in termination revealed that they had been held by 23 youth. Thus, of the 77 boys studied, over two-thirds (n=54) had never been fired from a job during their involvement in WAY.

In summary, with only a few exceptions, WAY scholars obtained a variety of employment experiences during their years in the program. Youth worked both on CV's campus at specially designed WAY worksites and at jobs they sought and obtained in the community. There was considerable variation in the proportion of jobs held on and off campus and in the proportion of time in the program during which youth worked. In order to bring to life some of these different patterns, following are case histories of youth who had very different employment experiences while in the WAY Scholarship program. For this purpose, three boys were selected: one who held many jobs, one with an average number of jobs, and one with few jobs.

> **WAY Employment Case History: Carlos (Ten jobs)**
>
> Carlos entered the WAY Scholarship program in January 1993 at age 14. The year before that he had been admitted to CV on a neglect petition after being found wandering the streets with his brothers. Reports were made that the mother (a known crack user and dealer) would put Carlos and his three brothers out of the house early in the morning and would not let them back in until 10:00 each night. The children did not have

proper clothing and resorted to begging on the street. While living on the campus at CV, Carlos worked at the Level 3 Village Store. Once inducted into WAY Scholarship, he obtained a Level 4 job at a local restaurant. From the beginning, his WAY counselor reported that Carlos' participation in WAY "has been excellent." His attitude was positive, and he was considered respectful and appropriate with adults and peers. That summer, things became more difficult for Carlos as he began to come to terms with the fact that his family could not accept him back. His social worker worked intensively with him as he struggled with whether to go to a foster home or a group home. He left his Level 4 job and stopped working for a while. In August a plan to move to a foster home was developed, and Carlos' attitude improved. He began working at the woodshop (a Level 3 job on campus) for a short while and then took some time off from work while he transitioned off campus to live with a foster family.

His second year of WAY Scholarship began with Carlos living at his foster home and not working during the school year. His WAY counselor reported, "Carlos is now a member of the T. family. He is enrolled in school and is a member of the basketball team. Carlos has been making friends and getting adjusted to family life." Later that winter his counselor continued to report a smooth transition, "I am extremely proud of Carlos. He is doing extremely well at his foster home, in school, and all around."

When the summer came he enrolled in the Summer Youth Employment Program and was assigned to work at a local college. In the fall, still living with the T. family, he took a few months off. As his counselor concluded, "With his school workload and the sports he's involved in, there wouldn't be much time for work." His counselor continued to support Carlos' adjustment into his foster family and new school and encouraged him to return to work when he was ready.

In his third year of WAY Scholarship, Carlos was ready to return to work and he applied for a job at a fish market/restaurant. He reported that he enjoyed work and was learning a lot. He received a promotion in March and increased his hours. In order to do so he had to give up being on the track team at school. His counselor reported that Carlos would be winning the WAY Scholarship work performance award that year and that he was "very proud of Carlos." In the fall Carlos left his job to focus on his varsity basketball and football. He proudly earned a starting position on the high school varsity football team and also made the high school basketball team. As long as his grades were good, it was decided he would not work while pursuing winter sports. But in the spring his biological mother reappeared, creating personal havoc for Carlos.

At the beginning of his fourth year of WAY Scholarship, Carlos was a senior in high school. Brief involvement with his mother was unsettling, though this "fizzled out" by January according to the counselor. Problems with his foster family surfaced, threatening to destroy all the progress Carlos had made. With the continued involvement of his WAY counselor, it was decided that Carlos would return to CV—not to the RTC, but to one of the agency's group homes. He accepted the change and made a good adjustment. It was arranged that Carlos would be bussed to the same school he had been attending, to help him maintain continuity in his life. As in past years, Carlos did not work during basketball season. In May his counselor reported that Carlos "went out and got his own job. He didn't need my help or guidance. He has become very resourceful in his job finding efforts." He began working at a local restaurant, but he was let go when there was not enough work for him. With his WAY counselor, Carlos went to the Department of Labor and got several job leads. Based on that effort, he obtained a job in a bakery. Carlos ended his fourth year in WAY Scholarship leaving the bakery job because of the long hours (12-hour days). His counselor told him to "hang in there even if he doesn't like a job or the hours. I told him he had to sacrifice until something better comes along."

In his final year in the WAY Scholarship program Carlos obtained work at a nearby Grand Union as a clerk and inventory specialist. He got off to a rocky start by not coming to work for 2 days while he was sick. Soon after, however, his counselor reported that "knowing that his stay at the group home was running out, [Carlos] decided to dramatically change his attitude to become a more positive person. He has become a role model." He signed up for training classes at Westchester Board of Cooperative

(Carlos' case history, continued)

Educational Services and began working part-time for a clothing manufacturer. He was reported to be a "very productive and reliable worker." After leaving that job, he took a full-time job at a nearby Dunkin Donuts. He remained there until the end of WAY. His hours increased significantly, and he was doing an excellent job. In his last month of WAY Scholarship Carlos was working 40 hours per week and "working his way up the company ladder." He was living at the YMCA in a nearby town and planning on taking college courses that fall.

WAY Employment Case History: Richard (Six jobs)

Richard was admitted to CV's RTC at age 11. He had been placed in a foster home at age 7 because of parental neglect. He had experienced a very difficult childhood, suffering many forms of maltreatment. Richard entered a CV group home 3 years later at age 14 and was recruited into WAY Scholarship at age 17. Upon enrollment in WAY Scholarship, Richard was in 11th grade. He was working at a custom clothing business making men's suits. During his first summer in WAY, Richard took a job at a summer day camp "in order to change scenery for a while." At the end of the summer he returned to making suits, earning $90 per week. His counselor reported having positive experiences with Richard.

He began his second year in WAY Scholarship by working and exploring options for college for the following year. At the WAY Scholarship dinner he received the Director's Award, and his counselor reported that Richard was "accepting more and more responsibility with the help of his employer, volunteer, and WAY counselor." That spring Richard graduated from high school and was accepted into a branch of City College. He worked throughout the summer and planned for college. But the transition to college was difficult for Richard, and he discontinued work at the end of his second year in WAY Scholarship to focus on his academics. His counselor reported that "Richard's concentration is currently on passing and appreciating his courses."

(Richard's case history, continued)

His third year of WAY Scholarship began with Richard doing a little better at school. His counselor reported that Richard "enjoys his teachers more and is determined to do well in school. He has discontinued work in order to focus on school." In the spring he moved into a CV-supervised independent living apartment and continued trying to pull up his grades. He was receiving tutoring and counseling at college, and he returned to his previous place of employment on a part-time basis. Yet, by summer he had been dismissed and then was reinstated to college on the condition that he maintain a "C" average. He completed his third year of WAY Scholarship working part-time and doing well at his job. Living in independent housing was posing some challenges, as Richard needed to learn how to maintain a household and budget while working and attending college.

He began the fourth year of WAY Scholarship by not working and focusing on maintaining his grades. At the same time he was faced with a major life decision, whether or not to relocate south with his family or to remain on his own in the New York City area. By the spring he had decided to remain in New York; he was still not working but his grades had improved. "Richard is maintaining a 'C' average and is looking forward to losing his probationary status," his counselor reported in the early summer. Richard returned to his previous place of employment. "The longevity of his job attests to his hard work and responsibility directed toward his work." He completed his fourth year of WAY "steady and reliable" with his employment, progressing slowly in college, and beginning to deal with his impending separation from CV when he turned 21.

Richard began his final year with WAY Scholarship working 30 hours a week at a new job as an outdoor messenger. Due to failing grades, he dropped out of college. Although his counselor encouraged him to reapply, Richard "was adamant about staying out of school for a semester so that he can save money and reestablish himself." Throughout the winter he worked as a messenger and lived in Queens in the independent living apartment. In the spring he reapplied for part-time status at college. His counselor reported, "He continues to be successfully employed at the messenger service; and he is well-liked for his work habits, especially his

(Richard's case history, continued)

record of dependability. He continues to save regularly." Upon returning to college, Richard felt better equipped to deal with the demands, with improved time management and studying skills. By summer Richard had been nominated for a promotion at work and had completed his first semester back at college. At the end of his final year in WAY Scholarship, Richard "continues to compile a stable work record and has earned the respect of his supervisor." He had made a good adjustment to indepen-

WAY Employment Case History: Kevin (Three jobs)

Kevin became a WAY scholar in January 1994, shortly after his 14th birthday, and 9 months after arriving at CV. For the first half-year in WAY Scholarship, he worked at the on-campus woodshop. An above-average reader and motivated worker, he appeared serious about the future and making long-term goals. Consequently, he was considered to be a promising candidate to hold an off-campus job. However, that step was delayed because Kevin was experiencing problems with peers at his cottage and seemed to have lost some momentum on the job, as well.

That summer, Kevin moved to the "transitional" CV group home located on the border of CV's campus. He did not work, as he adjusted to his new environment and anticipated a second move, to a group home in Queens. That subsequent off-campus placement was not wholly successful. Throughout the year, Kevin consistently cut classes and engaged in negative and confrontational behavior. His school performance slipped and, therefore, according to the rules of the group home, he was not allowed to hold a job.

After a year, he was transferred back to the transitional, near-campus group home. Soon, his behavior and school work stabilized. At that point, he was more interested in moving back to an off-campus group home than in seeking employment. Within a few months, he moved to a new CV group home, and he began a job search. His application to the Summer Youth Employment Program was rejected. As his WAY counselor noted, "There are simply too many kids and too few jobs."

With his counselor's assistance, Kevin brushed up on his interviewing and job search skills and was hired by McDonald's in his new community. However, he left the job before he had completed training. He again participated in numerous incidents that broke house rules. More serious offenses involving drugs and alcohol brought Kevin into the court system. As a result, instead of steering Kevin toward gainful employment, his WAY counselor arranged for Kevin to fulfill court-ordered community service. Continued disciplinary problems in the community led to Kevin's second return, at the end of 1996, to the group home bordering CV's campus.

After having lived in the community where he attended the local high school, 17-year-old Kevin was resentful about his return to the campus and to the on-site school. He also did not agree that he needed to enter a substance abuse rehabilitation program, for which he was awaiting placement. Overall, his negative attitude made it difficult for his WAY counselor to help Kevin develop a better work ethic. It was with some urging, then, that he took an on-campus job on CV's computer bus. However, he failed to attend the required training and soon abandoned that worksite.

Starting that summer—his fourth year in WAY Scholarship—Kevin made gradual progress in important areas of his life. After several months of efforts on the counselor's part, Kevin accepted a summer job at a local amusement park. At the same time, he attended school and counseling at a drug treatment center. In the fall, he returned to the off-campus group home and reenrolled in the public high school. He did well and earned his diploma the next June. That spring he began working at a restaurant in a local mall, a job he would hold for 6 months, until he entered college.

In summary, WAY youth gained employment experiences while on the campus of CV, in the local community surrounding CV, and in the communities to which they were discharged. On average, youths held just over four jobs; but employment varied depending in part on the many other factors that shaped the lives of these boys, including the extent of their long-standing emotional and behavioral problems. The WAY counselors played an active role in encouraging youth to work and to develop employment skills.

By the end of the program did WAY scholars have savings from their WAY employment?

♦ WAY scholars saved on average over $700.

WAY Scholarship youth were encouraged both to earn and to save money. In fact, saving money was one of the terms of the WAY contract. Saving was encouraged through a matched savings program; for every dollar saved, youth were eligible to receive a one-to-one match (up to $500 per year) to be used exclusively for college costs or vocational training. Youths with the highest savings record each year were also awarded a certificate at the annual WAY dinner, at which new scholars were inducted into the program and the accomplishments of current scholars were celebrated.

For the purpose of this study, savings were calculated as total dollars accumulated (personal and matched) at the end of the five-year program. This, of course, does not take into account any savings withdrawn prior to the end of the program. Nor does it take into account money youths saved in other accounts.[2] Yet, we believe that money saved as of the end of the program is a good estimate of a youth's ability to save money for his future (not just for a short period of time).[3] Table 8 presents the frequency distribution of total savings as of the end of the program (or just prior to withdrawing savings for college tuition). These data were available for all WAY Scholarship youth, cohorts 1 to 10.

As can be seen in Table 8, savings ranged from zero to just over $4,000 (actual highest savings was $4,001.49). Average savings at the end of the program was over $700 (Mean=$713.90, SD=$827.41).

---

2. All boys at CV have savings accounts for their allowances.
3. Some youth attended college before the end of the program. Their savings were calculated prior to college enrollment because the savings program was created to cover the costs of college tuition, which was deemed a legitimate reason to expend savings.

Table 8: Dollars Saved by WAY Scholars at the End of the 5-Year Program (Cohorts 1 to 10)

Total Dollars Saved	Valid N *	Valid %
$ 0	10	7.0%
1 to 250	46	32.4%
251 to 500	25	17.6%
551 to 750	14	9.9%
751 to 1000	12	8.5%
1001 to 2000	22	15.5%
2001 to 3000	9	6.3%
3001 to 4002	4	2.8%
TOTAL	**142**	**100%**

Mean = $713.90, SD = $827.41

* Missing data on 13 youth.

We also examined the comments made by the 39 WAY scholars (all of whom participated in WAY at least 2.5 years) who were interviewed as adults. In general, these remarks were very positive about the savings component of the program.

★ *Every dollar I put in they gave me a dollar for free.*

★ *The fact that you were saving money was emphasized and that was really cool.*

★ *I saved a little bit but not as much as they wanted me to. I knew it was a good idea. So it did work out that I saved some, but that savings is a real excellent program. It really is. I never took advantage of it.*

★ *The WAY program helped me budget my money and helped me save and think about the future.*

★ *The WAY program taught me how to save money, which is very important to me because I did not know how to save money. I used to get money and spend it, and then I used to have to ask my parents for more money. So now I know how to save, and I know what to do with that money.*

Scholars remembered with fondness how hard the counselors worked to help them save money.

★ *They kept bugging me so I just gave them the money.*

Upon reflection, most scholars admitted in the interview that they wished that they had saved more.

★ *I wished that I had saved more. The WAY program, they were trying to instill in me to push yourself, but I just didn't have the willingness in me to give them a fifty. I just didn't take advantage of it.*

★ *I did save money. It wasn't much though. I wish I could have saved a whole bunch more. When I was there the counselors matched me up with the donor match to try to get me to save more while I was in the group home. Unfortunately, I didn't have the chance to put anything away though, being in school and everything else.*

★ *The WAY program was like a bank. When you go to the bank and put a little bit of money in and they hold it for you and it doubles or whatever. That was a smart thing to do. I should have left my money in there and did it the right way, but I took it out.*

In summary, all but a few scholars had savings at the end of the 5-year program. Savings ranged from zero to just over $4,000, with average savings over $700. Most scholars interviewed felt that the savings was a very positive part of the program and appreciated the efforts that their counselors made to encourage them to save even more.

As young adults, were the WAY scholars employed?

◆ Of 39 youth interviewed as young adults, 80% were employed, 22 full-time.

◆ Full-time salaries among WAY scholars interviewed in 1996 and 1997 averaged $22,510.

During the extensive interviews with 39 (out of 64) WAY scholars from cohorts 1 through 6, information was obtained regarding current employment experiences (unemployed, working part-time, working full-time) and annual earnings for those working full-time. At the time of the interviews (1996–1997), these young men were between 21 and 30 years of age.

Eighty percent were employed at the time of the interview, 9 part-time and 22 full-time. Thus, of those young men working, 71% were working full-time and 29% were working part-time. Salaries were examined for the 22 employed full-time. Annual salaries ranged from $10,712 to $57,200, with a mean of $22,510 and a median of $18,532. The mean earnings for these WAY scholars—a subsample that could be reached and that agreed to be interviewed—was the same as the national average for high school graduates (U.S. Census Bureau 1997). Through discussions with these young men, it was learned that most had worked intermittently since leaving CV (during and after WAY Scholarship), experimenting with various employment settings and work schedules. Some had settled down into salaried jobs at banks, retail businesses, or public service jobs; others were paid by the hour as furniture movers, construction workers, or in fast-food settings. Most participants exhibited a strong work history that began with the WAY program and carried forward from the time they left CV through their early adulthood. The following three case histories illustrate the types of issues WAY scholars faced in trying to gain employment experiences in the years during and following discharge from CV.

Adult Employment Case Study: Curtis

Curtis came to CV in 1983 as a 13-year-old Latino boy with a history of being physically abused and neglected. He was a sad and angry boy, exhibiting both suicidal tendencies as well as violent outbursts. His natural father was an abusive man, only intermittently involved with his family. At age 15 Curtis was recruited into the first cohort of the WAY Scholarship program. At the time he was involved with WAY Works in a Level 3 job at CV's warehouse. He performed his job well and received promotions along the way. For a while he had a newspaper route that he went to every morning, leaving his RTC cottage at 5:00 a.m. He later worked at a local gas station and at an auto parts store. Curtis made the most of his WAY Scholarship employment opportunities and continued working even as he moved off campus and experienced several changes in residence in the ensuing years.

(Curtis' case study, continued)

After a move to his mother's in 1987, Curtis took an after-school job at a shoe store, starting out in stock and then moving to sales. Things did not work out at home, primarily because of his mother's psychiatric problems; and Curtis was moved back to CV's transitional group home in 1989. Some time later Curtis returned to his mother's. "At first it was kind of hard finding work. So I had a few part-time jobs. I worked in a deli and at the gas station on the weekends. For a short time I went through a couple of different jobs—vacuum salesman, Dollar Rent-A-Car." His first full-time job came in 1990 as a sheet metal worker, working for a few different construction companies. In April 1992, the New York City Taxi and Limousine Service Commission hired Curtis as a peace officer. He received on-the-job training and maintained that job up until the time of the interview in 1996. At that time his annual salary was $32,000. It is clear from this record that Curtis worked consistently and was able to maintain a strong employment history, even as he moved residences and sampled different career options.

Adult Employment Case Study: Jorge

Jorge was admitted to CV in 1985 at age 11, having been neglected at home and physically abused by his mother's boyfriend. He lived in a violent and gang-infested neighborhood. Jorge presented as an angry boy who claimed he wanted to retaliate for the abuse both he and his mother had experienced. He also showed signs of suicidal behavior including thoughts about jumping off a rooftop.

In 1988 at age 14, he was recruited into the 3rd cohort of the WAY Scholarship program. He was living on the campus of CV and working as an administrative assistant. He also worked for a while on the computer bus. In 1990 he was discharged to his mother's home in the Bronx. His WAY counselor noted that Jorge needed consistent support because his family did not see the value of his completing school or working. Shortly after, his mother moved out, leaving him alone. In order to pay the bills he began dealing drugs, earning $3,000 a day. "Nothing I am proud of," said Jorge. "I did what I had to do. I had no way to take care of myself; I was still young at the time." The following year he moved to Buffalo to make a clean start. He lost all of his money and ended up in the hospital with pneumonia. From a distance, his WAY counselor attempted to maintain contact through letters and phone calls both to Jorge and through various contacts. In August 1991, Jorge was considered officially dropped from the program after 6 months of no contact.

When interviewed more than 6 years later, Jorge filled in the missing pieces of his life since leaving WAY Scholarship. When Jorge recovered from his illness, he moved to Pennsylvania to live with his aunt. He stayed there for 2 years, working at a bakery for 6 months earning $5.25 per hour. "Legal money, slow money" according to Jorge. He packed ice for a year at $6 per hour. This was followed by a full-time job at Wendy's for $4.95 per hour for 4 months. His next job was at Lehigh Valley Downs racetrack. He started off as a dishwasher, was promoted to prep cook, and then finally became a chef. He was earning $6.25 per hour. A roofing company was his next place of employment, until it went bankrupt. For the next 6 months he worked in a temporary agency, doing shipping and receiving. In October 1997 he began working at another company, also in shipping and receiving, for $7 per hour. At the time of the interview, he was hopeful that he would be hired there on a permanent basis and that his salary would be raised to $11 per hour. "I'm going to be a driver for them. They're going to hire me permanently. I get 401k, all medical benefits, my salary will go up to $11 per hour and as the years go, it will go up even more." Jorge was hopeful about his future. "I'm proud of myself," he explained, for living a decent life.

Adult Employment Case Study: Chester

Chester was admitted to CV in 1984 at age 13. His mother was crippled and blind from multiple sclerosis and could no longer take care of him. He had a history of neglect as well as behavioral problems including truancy, violent behavior, and destruction of property. His father had not been involved with him since his infancy. At age 14 Chester joined the first cohort of the WAY Scholarship program. He worked on the campus in the grounds department. He enjoyed working and credited the WAY Scholarship program with teaching him the importance of employment. "I just try to picture my life if I didn't go to WAY. If I had turned down WAY would I be used to working? I would probably say 'no' because when I got home I started working pretty quick." He elaborated that it was the "work habits, what you learned about working, you learned from the Village, being in the WAY program." Soon after being discharged, he got a job working with mentally retarded children. At the time of the interview, 6 years later, he was still working at the same place. "It just grows on you," Chester explained, "I really know what I am doing." He concluded by explaining how the WAY program helped him learn how to be a good employee. "The hardest part about working is working with others. I think that is what I learned in the WAY program, is working with others. So when I got out into the real world I knew exactly what I had to do." Chester clearly incorporated the positive work ethics so central to the WAY program, "I always tried to be the best worker I could be, I always tell my present employers, you can always back track on the records because all these guys want me back. There's only one job I left because I wasn't happy. The rest of the jobs that I had, everybody still wants me back to this day."

7 ■■■■■■■■■■■■■■■■■■■■■■■■■■■■

Findings: Did WAY Scholars Achieve Educational Success?

By the end of the program, were WAY scholars educational achievers?

♦   At the end of the 5-year program, 81% of the WAY scholars who participated in the program for at least 2.5 years (76% of the participants) were still in school or had graduated.

High school completion—either by the end of the program or by age 21—was one of the most important outcomes assessed in this study. WAY Scholarship was based on the belief that school success and early employment experiences are key for successful adult employment. High school graduation represents a foundation for one-half of that equation. Keeping youth in school and helping them navigate their way to graduation was a very important part of the WAY scholar-counselor relationship. School status was assessed for WAY Scholarship cohorts 1 to 10 after 5 years of enrollment. These data were collected from exit interviews with youth and from bimonthly WAY counselor reports and were available for youth who participated in WAY Scholarship at least 2.5 years—three-fourths of the participants. These data are presented in Table 9.

At the end of the program only 9 out of 118 scholars (8%) were school dropouts (had dropped out of high school before graduation and were not enrolled in a GED program). Just over one-third (n=44, 37%) were still attending high school or were enrolled in a GED program. Eighteen (15%) had graduated or received a GED, and 34 (29%) had attended or were still in college.

Taken together, 81% of the scholars who participated for at least 2.5 years were educational achievers at the end of the WAY Scholarship program. They had graduated from high school, received their GEDs, or were still enrolled in school. Over one-quarter (29%) had gone on to college. In contrast, only 9 boys were known to have dropped

Table 9: Educational Achievement at the End of the 5 Years for WAY Scholars (Cohorts 1 to 10) Who Completed at Least 2.5 Years in the Program

School Status at End of 5 years	N *	%
Achievers	**96**	**81%**
In HS/GED Program	44	37%
Completed HS/GED	52	44%
Received GED	5	4%
HS Diploma	13	11%
Some College	12	10%
In College	22	19%
Others	**22**	**19%**
HS Dropout	9	8%
No Information	13	11%
TOTAL	**118**	**100%**

* Educational attainment data for 37 youth who completed less than 2.5 years were unavailable at the 5-year point; they are excluded from this table.

out of high school without graduating or earning a GED, and for another 13 boys (11%) educational status could not be determined. The 13 scholars with unknown school status were considered nonachievers in these analyses, resulting in a conservative estimate of educational achievement at the end of the program. It is unlikely that all 15 of these youth were nonachievers. If any were school achievers, the rate of achievement would be higher than 81%.

In addition, the educational status of the WAY scholars who participated in the program for less than 2.5 years (n=37) remains unknown. If all of these youth were nonachievers, the educational achievement rate could be as low as 62%. This is, however, an unlikely scenario. Conversely, if all 37 youth were achievers—also unlikely—the achievement rate would be as high as 86%. No matter how one looks at it, the proportion of achievers is impressive, even more so given the multitude of obstacles the WAY scholars faced in their backgrounds and the subsequent efforts required to complete their education. The following two case histories illustrate some of these challenges.

Educational Achievement Case Study: Jesus

Jesus was inducted into WAY Scholarship in 1992 at age 14. He had been physically abused by his father and was an angry and violent boy. He had a history of truancy, aggressive behavior, theft, and destruction of property. He was in 9th grade at the special education public school situated on CV's campus. He was working at a nearby gas station for his Level 4 job, and he was the captain of the basketball team. Academically, his counselor viewed him as "not a problem," but someone who needed some tutoring and some help with his schoolwork. He received good grades that spring (mostly "A's" and "B's"), and his counselor reported that "he continues to do well in school." Jesus was sent home on trial discharge to his mother, and he transferred to a technical high school. His first year of WAY Scholarship ended at a point where he was evidencing difficulty accepting his mother's authority but doing "exceptionally well in school."

It soon became apparent that Jesus's transition home "was not a success," and this affected his schoolwork. He transferred to a different school but was later suspended. Eventually he moved to Queens to live with his uncle. At first the move was positive and Jesus attended summer school to prepare for another new school, near his new residence. A reduction in disruptive behavior led to a good beginning for Jesus, and his grades for the fall semester were not bad. But by the winter he was having problems with his uncle, who was considering terminating the living arrangements. Again, Jesus's school performance suffered. He failed two subjects. By the summer, Jesus had moved again, this time to live with his long-time volunteer and possible foster parent. According to his counselor's reports, once Jesus made this move, his school performance improved dramatically, and he settled down into a positive relationship with his foster father. From that point forward, Jesus's schoolwork was fine. "Jesus continues to do well. He plays on the school's football team and is trying out for the basketball team. The new environment is working very well for Jesus; and his foster father, Jim, has helped Jesus focus on his school, job, and future plans." At the end of his third year in WAY, his counselor reported, "When one compares this year with the previous year in Jesus's life, it is like night and day. Jesus, since his move upstate with

(Jesus' case history, continued)

his foster father, has shown significant improvements in his schoolwork and at home. He is much more positive about his future and is not involved in fights or having any disciplinary problems at home or in the community. Credit should be given to the foster father for his effort in giving Jesus this positive image of himself."

In his last 2 years of WAY Scholarship, Jesus transferred to a regular high school, graduated, and began community college. He received the personal growth trophy at the annual WAY dinner. The last report made by the counselor noted that, although Jesus did not do as well in college as he would have liked, he hoped to improve the next year and "he remains positive about college and has a desire to do well." It is clear from the chronology of events that Jesus's school problems were directly linked to his living arrangements. The WAY counselor provided the constancy and the glue between these many transitions; and once he was settled into a positive home environment with his foster father, his schoolwork improved. It is also noteworthy that since leaving CV, Jesus attended four different high schools, a common pattern among older youth in the child welfare system.

Educational Achievement Case Study: Roger

Roger began WAY Scholarship in January 1992 at age 13.5. He was living in a CV group home and attending 8th grade. One month later he left the group home and returned to live with his mother in Brooklyn. Shortly after that he ran away from home, and because of the advocacy of the WAY counselor he was referred to a CV group home in Queens. He began a new school that spring. He joined the school choir and began performing for audiences. According to his counselor, Roger was doing well in school and had adjusted to the new group home, although he was engaged in a conflict with another resident. In the fall he began 9th

(Roger's case history, continued)

grade. However, by October personal problems were creating difficulties for him at the group home; he began cutting classes and coming to school late. "Roger's adjustment to the group home is not going well. He seems to be upset about something that he refuses to discuss." At the end of his first year in WAY Scholarship, Roger was expressing some interest in returning to his mother; meanwhile, his counselor and other staff believed that he should be transferred to an adolescent RTC. "Roger is conflicted by his pull to return to his family and their unwillingness to accept him wholly."

The beginning of his second year in WAY Scholarship, Roger returned to his first CV group home and began school on the campus of CV. However, because of his anger toward the agency, it was believed that he might do better in a totally new environment. In the early spring, Roger was transferred to a different RTC. He began attending school on the campus of the other RTC. He remained in contact with his WAY counselor. "We are hopeful that he will be able to resolve some of the more complex clinical issues while he is in this setting," his counselor wrote. His mother was making plans to move to Alabama at that time, and this caused conflict for Roger who wanted to be with her. The counselor noted that he strongly believed that this would not be a positive move. Things settled down for Roger; he did not return to his mother, and he finished the school year. The more restrictive setting was apparently a positive experience for him. However, the WAY counselor noted that the school's standards were not particularly high. Roger was still being considered for discharge to his mother "as soon as she moved from her present community."

Roger began his third year in WAY Scholarship still living at the other RTC and attending school there. His counselor reported, "Roger continues to do well in school." Roger was seeing his family regularly, and the plan for discharge was still under discussion. At the end of the school year Roger moved to another group home in a nearby town and began attending the local high school. He got off to a bad start and was suspended for 3 days. His counselor reported that Roger could do well in school but believed that the previous school did not provide him with the proper education. His counselor arranged for him to receive tutoring to catch up. At the same time, Roger began visiting his mother in Brooklyn, which led to problems in the community including some trouble with the law.

In the spring Roger began cutting classes, resulting in poor grades. He was suspended for bad behavior and was held back. The counselor report stated that, "Roger has been having difficulties in the group home and at school. He was suspended from school twice in April and once in May. The group home tried to plan with Roger to overcome his difficulties, but Roger left without their consent. Efforts are being made to contact [him]." In his last report the following month, the counselor noted that Roger dropped out of high school and out of the WAY Scholarship program. "All attempts to change his mind have failed." Thus, the WAY counselor could not sway Roger onto a better path. The negative influence of his mother's problems and the community in which she lived could not be overcome by the program.

Pursuing an Education: In Their Own Words

Transcripts of the interviews with WAY youth conducted several years after the end of the program were also enlightening. These interviews revealed the types of struggles the young men faced as they tried to complete their high school education. One theme that emerged in the interviews was the need for greater structure than was sometimes provided by their families. Some youth felt that without the external support supplied by WAY they would not have completed their education.

> ★ *I became quite a little truant. I got in touch with [the Executive Director of CV] and I spoke to her about coming back to the Village because I knew that I wanted to get in my present field and I had to get at least a high school diploma. So I knew I wasn't going to be able to do it on my own because I was very headstrong and my mother was not very good as a disciplinarian so I needed some guidance. I needed a structured environment.*

★   *Problems that might occur along the way, they help you out. Any questions about school or anything to further your education, they are willing to go the extra amount to get information for you, just to see the best possible route to succeed in your education.*

★   *At one point I wanted to go home, but it didn't seem like the right place to be with my mother because I knew I wouldn't finish high school if I went home.*

★   *I was very determined to go to parochial school...in order to get a good education and the discipline and that type of thing. I knew I would need a lot of structure because I still did have a behavioral problem so I thought Catholic school would be the best thing for me.*

Did educational achievement rates improve from the end of the program to age 21?

The following statistics apply to youth in cohorts 1 to 6 who had participated in WAY for at least 2.5 years (71% of the youth):

◆   At age 21, 80% of WAY scholars were still in school or had already graduated; almost one-third of the youth were enrolled in college.

◆   Four of the eight youth who had dropped out of high school by the end of the program reenrolled by age 21.

◆   Four of the seven youth who had dropped out of college by the end of the program reenrolled by age 21.

◆   Youth needed more than 4 years to complete their high school education. Seventy-two percent of those still in school at the end of the 5-year program went on to complete high school by age 21.

School completion after 4 years of entering high school was an inaccurate measure of ultimate school achievement for these youth. Citywide data suggest that this holds true for other groups of teenagers as well.[1] Disadvantaged and at-risk youth—like WAY schol-

---

1. The New York City Board of Education (1996) found that an additional 13.1% of Latino students and 21.9% of black students earned high school diplomas in the 3 years after their 1993 expected date of graduation.

ars—frequently do not complete high school within 4 years. They may need an additional 2 or 3 years to make up for long-standing academic or attendance difficulties. In addition, WAY scholars tended to move around several times after discharge from CV, so it might have taken them longer than those with greater stability to complete high school.

By age 21, WAY scholars had left foster care and were no longer eligible for public education. Most scholars had several additional years to complete school if they were behind in grade level, and those who left school had some time to decide whether they would return. For these reasons, educational achievement at age 21 was chosen as an appropriate time to assess long-term educational outcomes for WAY scholars. It also allowed for a comparison of educational achievement of scholars at two points in time (at the end of the WAY program and at age 21). It was expected that the educational achievement rates would be higher at age 21 because scholars had more time to achieve the goal of completing a high school level education.

In the current analyses only cohorts 1 to 6 were included because those are the cohorts for whom we have data at both points in time. Table 10 compares the educational achievement of these six cohorts at the end of the program with the achievement of the same scholars at 21 years of age. For these analyses, data were available only for youths who participated in at least 2.5 years of the program. There were 64 scholars in cohorts 1 to 6 (data for two were not analyzed because the youth died in car accidents after the end of the program but before the age of 21).

As Table 10 indicates, the number of scholars who were educational achievers at age 21 was virtually identical to the number of educational achievers at the end of the program. Just 20% or so were either high school dropouts or were missing information on their school status at both points in time.[2] This effect occurred because those still in school at the end of the program were already considered achievers, even though many went on to higher levels of achievement by obtaining a high school diploma or GED and by attending college.

---

2. School status information was obtained from various sources: exit interviews with the youth at the end of the program, bimonthly reports filled out by the WAY counselors during their involvement with the program, correspondence with the youth, CV staff who knew the educational status of the youth, alumni interviews conducted with 39 cohort 1 through 6 scholars in 1997, or from recent surveys filled out by the scholars. Independent attempts were not made by CV's research department to confirm school attendance and graduation. But WAY counselors were often in contact with guidance counselors and teachers, and sometimes they attended graduations. In addition, the WAY program often assisted with college applications and provided financial assistance for college. Consequently, counselors did not usually need to depend on the word of the scholar regarding his educational status.

Table 10: Educational Achievement at the End of the 5 Years and at Age 21 for Scholars Who Completed At Least 2.5 Years in the WAY Program (Cohorts 1 to 6)

School Status	End of WAY		Age 21	
	N	%	N	%
Achievers	*52*	*81%*	*51*	*80%*
In HS/GED Program	24	38%	2	3%
Completed HS/GED	28	44%	49	77%
HS Grad/GED	10	16%	22	34%
Some College	7	11%	8	13%
In College	11	17%	19	30%
Others	*12*	*19%*	*13*	*20%*
HS Dropout	8	13%	7	11%
No Information	4	6%	6	9%
TOTAL	*64*	*100%*	*64*	*100%*

Although the total numbers of achievers and nonachievers remained stable at both points in time, there were changes within the categories of various levels of achievement. At the end of the program, 24 youth (38%) were still in school, whereas at age 21 there were just 2 scholars (3%) still in school. Many of those in school at the end of the program obtained their degree by age 21, an increase from 28 youth (44%) at the end of the program to 49 youth (77%) at age 21. These data substantiate the argument that certain groups of youth need more than 4 years to complete their secondary education.

Another important change from the end of the program to age 21 was the increase in college attendance. While the number of college dropouts increased only by 1 (from 7 to 8 youth), the number currently attending college increased from 11 youth (17%) at the end of the program to 19 youth (30%) at age 21. Thus, in the years between the end of the program and age 21, there was a substantial jump in the number of scholars completing high school and attending college.

It was also of interest to see how many nonachievers returned to school by age 21. Results revealed that of the 8 high school dropouts at the end of the program, 4 (50%) had gone back to school by age 21. Three were still dropouts, and 1 had missing educational data at age 21. Although these numbers are small, the data suggest that there was some fluidity in school status over time. Dropping out of school at the end of the program was not necessarily an indication that a scholar would never finish. In fact, half of the dropouts returned to school by age 21. Similarly, of the 7 youth who had dropped out of college by the end of the program, 4 had returned by age 21. Again, youth used the time between the end of the program and turning 21 to refocus themselves on educational goals. The fewest changes occurred among the 10 young men who had completed high school (two with a GED) by the end of the program. Only 1 of these youth went on to pursue higher education by age 21.

Did the WAY youth have higher educational attainment rates than the comparison youth at the end of the program?

♦ Eighty-two percent of the WAY Scholarship youth who remained in the program at least 2.5 years attained the status of educational achiever at the end of the 5-year program, versus just 66% of those not dropping out of the comparison group. This difference was statistically significant.

♦ For the 2 groups as a whole, although not statistically significant, differences in educational achievement rates between WAY Scholarship and comparison youth ranged from 6% to 17%, with WAY youth consistently achieving higher rates of educational success.

The strategy for analyzing educational data entailed two approaches. First we compared the youth in WAY Scholarship who remained involved for at least half the program with the youth in the comparison group who did not drop out of the study. Next, we looked at all of the WAY Scholars, including study dropouts and all of the comparison youth.

First, the educational achievement of youth in the first 6 cohorts who remained in the program for at least 2.5 years (71% of the enrollees) was compared to the educational achievement of youth who did not drop out of the comparison group. A youth was considered to be an achiever if he was in school at the end of the program or had already graduated from high school or earned an equivalency degree. In contrast, a nonachiever was a youth who left school before earning a degree. In addition, for the purpose of this particular analysis, youth who had unknown educational status as of the end of the 5-year program were considered nonachievers. Four of the 66 WAY participants had missing educational achievement at the end of the program (6%), versus four of the 61 comparison group youth (7%).

The educational achievement rate of WAY scholars in cohorts 1 through 6 was 82%.[3] That is to say, 82% of those who stuck with the program for at least 2.5 years either graduated from school or were still in school five years after program enrollment. In contrast, the educational achievement rate of the comparison group was just 66% (Table 11). This 16% difference in educational achievement rates between WAY youth and the comparison group is statistically significant (Chi-square [n=127]=4.35, p < .05). Consequently, being a WAY scholar was associated with higher rates of educational achievement than being a member of the comparison group.

Next, educational achievement rates were compared for WAY Scholarship cohorts 1 to 6 and comparison cohorts 1 to 6 for the groups as a whole, regardless of participation rates. These analyses included all youth enrolled into each of the two groups. In both groups, a significant portion (about one-third) did not have educational achievement data available at the end of the program. Thus, there was too much missing data to be able to have confidence in computations of actual achievement rates. However, because the percent of missing data was distributed evenly between groups, we created four estimates of the difference in achievement rates to answer the question of whether the educational achievement rate in the WAY Scholarship group was higher than in the comparison group. Thus, four different ways of coding missing data were used in order to explore the range of possible differences in educational achievement between the two groups. The results are reported in Table 12.

In the first approach, we eliminated missing data from both groups, resulting in WAY Scholarship achievement rates 17% higher than the comparison group. Coding missing data as nonachievers resulted in WAY achievement rates 6% higher than the comparison group. A third method was to project that 80% of the missing data in each group would actually be coded as achievers, resulting in WAY Scholarship achievement rates 12% higher than comparison youth. And finally, if we applied the known percentages of achievers in each group to the missing data, WAY Scholarship achievement rates would

---

3. This achievement rate differs from the rate reported in Table 10 because it includes two youths who were educational achievers at the end of the program, but died in car accidents before turning 21.

Table 11: Cross-Tabulation of Educational Achievement: WAY Scholarship Versus Comparison Youth (Cohorts 1 to 6)

	WAY > 2.5 Years	Comparison Youth Nondropouts	Total
Nonachiever	12	21	33
Column %	18%	34%	26%
Achiever	54	40	94
Column %	82%	66%	74%
Total	66	61	127

Table 12: WAY Scholars' Differential Advantage in Educational Achievement Compared to the Comparison Group (Cohorts 1 to 6) at the End of the Program Under Four Scenarios for Treating Missing Data

Treatment of Missing Data	Percentage of WAY's Advantage in Achievement
Removed from both groups	17%
Coded as nonachievers in both groups	6%
Coded as 80% achievers and 20% nonachievers	12%
Coded as same percentage of achievers and nonachievers as within each group.	17%
	Mean = 13%

be 17% higher than the comparison group. Although no one approach was foolproof given the high percentage of missing data, we can have confidence that in each case the WAY Scholarship youth had higher rates of achievement than the comparison youth and that these differences lay between 6% to 17%. Thus, if 100 youth enrolled in WAY Scholarship and 100 youth enrolled in the comparison group, between 6 and 17 more boys would be educational achievers in the WAY Scholarship group than in the comparison group. We consider this to be a meaningful finding, although none of the chi-squares were statistically significant.

By age 21, did educational achievement rates of the WAY scholars compare favorably to national rates?

For the three-fourths of the youth who participated in WAY for at least 2.5 years,

◆ WAY scholars' achievement rates were on a par with national graduation rates for all students and were substantially better than national rates for Latino youth, New York City rates for black and Latino youth, New York City special education rates, and national rates for youth in poverty.

As discussed earlier, the educational achievement rate for WAY scholars who completed at least 2.5 years of WAY Scholarship was about 80%. This was the case whether the achievement rate included cohorts 1 to 10 at the end of program, cohorts 1 to 6 at the end of program, or cohorts 1 to 6 at age 21. The comparison group was created so that WAY youth could be compared to their peers. We also wanted to compare our data to those of other studies, but it was difficult to find another study that provides education rates that are truly comparable to WAY rates. This is partly due to the dearth of longitudinal studies of youth in residential treatment. One of the few relevant studies reported a graduation rate of 71% for those who were discharged from foster care group settings (Festinger 1983).[4] Yet, this sample was based primarily on youth who were discharged from group homes or foster boarding homes rather than RTCs. Another study reported a high school graduation rate of 63% among those discharged after turning 19 years of age. This study contained a substantial amount of missing information (13%) and did not differentiate between school dropouts and those still in school (Westat 1989, pp. 4–17). Thus, the data are not useful for comparative purposes. Likewise, another phase

---

4. This was a study of 269 young adults who were interviewed at 23 to 26 years of age who had been discharged from foster care group settings (Festinger 1983).

of that study reported that 54% of the discharged foster care population between the ages of 18 to 24 had completed high school (Westat 1991), an age range younger than the one we used. Thus, it was difficult to find an educational achievement rate for a group that is truly comparable to the circumstances of WAY scholars.

Figure 1 presents the educational achievement rates for cohorts 1 to 6 WAY scholars at age 21 in comparison with city and national norms and other relevant comparison groups.[5] The figures used for comparison include graduation rates for Latino youth nationwide, New York City black and Latino students, New York City special education classes, and youth in poverty nationwide.

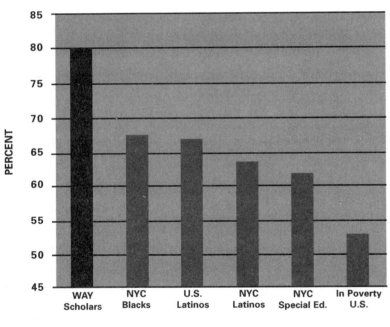

Figure 1: Educational Achievement Rates

5. The WAY educational achievement rate of 80% is based on the proportion of youth in cohorts 1 to 6 at age 21 who were high school graduates or who had completed a GED, were in a GED program, or were still in school (Table 10). The national graduation rates are based on U.S. Census data (Federal Interagency Forum on Child and Family Statistics 1999). These graduates include all persons between the ages of 18 to 24 who received a diploma or an equivalent alternative credential obtained by passing exams such as the GED exam. The New York City graduation rates are from the Board of Education (1996) and are based on a 3-year follow-up study of the class of 1993. Achievement rates for those between the ages of 18 to 24 in the general population living below the poverty level in 1997 who had completed high school is reported in Westat (1991).

As can be seen in Figure 1, achievement rates for WAY scholars were substantially higher than national Latino graduation rates (67%), New York City rates for either blacks (68%) or Latinos (64%), New York City special education rates (62%), and higher than national rates among youth in poverty (53%). These data are particularly impressive given the many barriers to educational achievement faced by the WAY scholars. Youth who are in care at CV are some of the most troubled youth in the New York City child welfare system, experiencing multiple risk factors for school failure such as poverty, learning disabilities, behavioral problems, and traumatic family disruptions.

Despite these impressive high school graduation rates, the WAY scholars did not fare as well in college. Although we did not have educational attainment data on all youth beyond the age of 21, we could determine some trends from the interviews with 39 of the WAY scholars (cohorts 1 to 6). Of the 19 youth in college at age 21, interviews were available for 14 of them. By the time of the interview, 10 had left college, 3 were still enrolled, and 1 had graduated with a bachelor's degree. Thus, at least half of the 19 youth had dropped out of college (10 out of 19), and the number could be higher if the other college attendees (those not interviewed) at age 21 also dropped out.

The interview comments are suggestive of some of the obstacles scholars faced in pursuing higher education. Some youth commented that they simply were not prepared for the academic and social demands of college.

★ *In high school I didn't have good study habits. I found that by not maintaining some kind of study pattern, you're not going to get anywhere and at first I didn't see that. I found out that it [college] was a whole different ball game, but I thought I could take on the work that they gave me. And I thought my mind was strong enough to withstand the college atmosphere, the parties. The reason I stopped going was because I knew I was jeopardizing myself.*

★ *The motivation wasn't there. It's nothing like high school, and it's nothing like junior high. Everything is on you because you're paying for it.*

★ *Academically I was ready. I just wasn't focused.*

Other youth described the personal forces in their lives—some positive and some negative—that interfered with their college plans.

★ *The bottom line was trying to get out of my mother's house. I planned on moving from there but I did everything wrong. I was concerned about leaving I* *didn't think what I was doing, and I dropped three very important classes from school; but I dropped late so I had to pay a penalty. I owed the school over $700, and that is what stopped me from going back.*

★ *I was enrolled in New York Tech on a basketball scholarship. I got into an accident and hurt my finger so I lost the scholarship.*

★ *I didn't complete Pace Business School. I went there for about 14 months out of 18 months and met my future wife. I kind of got sidetracked. I said, "Well, I can finish up when I go into the military," and when I got in I just never followed up on that, with me working nights and with the duty time.*

A third theme for these youth was the high cost of attending college and the difficulty of navigating the financial aid system.

★ *I went to New Haven on a basketball scholarship. The first year of college the experience is unbelievable. I didn't like the school very much. I took a semester off and went to a school that recruited me. But my financial aid form sat on a shelf of my house for a semester, and I lost aid. I ended up having to owe New Haven $2,000 for them to release my transcripts. I had an unofficial copy and Caldwell actually let me into the school without my transcript. That whole time I was working on getting my transcripts, I was maintaining 12 to 15 credits per semester and maintaining a job, but I wasn't allowed to play basketball. In addition to owing New Haven money, I had a bill at Caldwell. The next semester I had to take off because Caldwell is a very expensive school.*

These qualitative data strongly suggest that the WAY Scholarship youth, although highly motivated to attend college, may need more external support and structure to be able to complete their higher education.

8

■ ■

Findings: Did WAY Scholars Prepare for Self-Sufficiency?

By the end of the program, were WAY scholars on a self-sufficiency trajectory?

♦ Over 95% of WAY scholars who had participated for at least 2.5 years in WAY Scholarship were on a self-sufficiency trajectory at the end of the program (they were either in school, working, or had obtained high school or equivalency degrees). According to a more conservative measure, 85% were considered to be on a self-sufficiency trajectory.

The WAY Scholarship program was designed primarily to assist at-risk youth in leading self-sufficient and productive lives. To that end, through ongoing contact with the WAY counselor, each scholar was encouraged to stay in school and to find work experiences. As they progressed through the program, scholars obtained work experiences that allowed them to explore potential career interests and were offered support and tools to help them stay in and graduate from high school. At the end of 5 years, all scholars were over 18 years of age, an important time in a young person's life. With the program winding down, the five-year point was a meaningful time to ascertain whether these young men were on a self-sufficiency trajectory.

In this study self-sufficiency was examined in two ways. First, youth were considered to be on a self-sufficiency trajectory if they were educational achievers (in school or already obtained high school credentials) or if they were employed at the end of the program. Thus, according to this first conceptualization of self-sufficiency, a high school graduate or a GED recipient was considered to be on a self-sufficiency trajectory even if he was unemployed. Likewise, if a youth had dropped out of high school but was employed, he was considered to be on a self-sufficiency trajectory. For several reasons, we considered high school or equivalency graduates to be self-sufficient even if they were not in school or working at the end of the WAY Scholarship program. First, not all youth were able to find good jobs immediately after finishing school, but at least they had obtained credentials that would allow them entry into the labor market. Youth at the end of the program were still young enough that they were likely not to have been on a secure career path; thus, periods of unemployment were to be expected. Furthermore, youth might have changed jobs frequently; they may have been between jobs at the five-year point.

Using this broad conceptualization of self-sufficiency, WAY scholars did extraordinarily well. Of the 103 scholars from cohorts 1 to 10 who had participated in the program for at least 2.5 years and for whom information was available,[1] over 95% (n=98) were on a self-sufficiency trajectory, meaning that they were either in school, working, or had obtained high school or equivalency degrees. Only 5 youth were not on a self-sufficiency trajectory.

We also created a more conservative measure of self-sufficiency. According to this measure, only youth in school or employed at the end of the program were coded as being on a self-sufficiency trajectory. Thus, high school graduates and GED recipients were considered self-sufficient only if they were also employed. Consequently, everyone in this category was actively engaged in productive activity at either school or work at the end of the 5-year program.

Using this second definition of self-sufficiency, the vast majority of scholars were still coded as being on a self-sufficiency trajectory. That is, about 85% of the scholars for whom their status could be determined were self-sufficient. In contrast, just 15% were neither in school nor employed at the end of the program.[2] Thus, looking at self-sufficiency in 2 different ways, the majority of WAY youth after 5 years of the program were on a self-sufficiency trajectory.

Was residence related to being on a self-sufficiency trajectory at the end of the program?

♦ Neither discharge destination from CV's campus nor residence at the end of the program was statistically associated with a self-sufficiency trajectory for youth who participated in at least 2.5 years of WAY.

---

1. Self-sufficiency status could not be determined for 15 youth whose educational or employment data as of the end of the program were not known.

The importance of having a high school or equivalency diploma or being on a path to obtaining one by the end of the program cannot be overemphasized. A basic education provides both the skills and credentials to compete for jobs. Having a job can also help support the long-term goal of self-sufficiency for youth not in school. Many scholars were both in school and employed at the end of the program; others were not. We felt it was important to try to understand why some youth were not on a self-sufficiency trajectory at the end of the program.

One factor that might have influenced whether youth were on a self-sufficiency trajectory at the end of the program was residence, both the one to which the scholar was discharged after CV and the one where he may have been several years later at the end of the 5-year program. We began by exploring whether residence at discharge (discharge destination) from the campus of CV was associated with self-sufficiency. The discharge destination was identified for 100 scholars in cohorts 1 to 10 (the 13 scholars who were living in group homes at the time of enrollment in WAY Scholarship and the 5 who were enrolled from foster homes were excluded from this analysis). Discharge destination was categorized as a structured group setting (group home, RTC, Job Corps) or family environment (birth family, foster family, adoptive family). For these analyses, the more conservative measure of self-sufficiency was used in order to increase the variability.

As can be seen in Table 13, over half (56%) of the scholars were discharged to structured group settings from CV's RTC, mostly group homes. Forty-three percent were discharged to family environments, mostly birth and kinship families. These data allowed us to ask if discharge destination was associated with whether or not a youth was on a self-sufficiency trajectory at the end of the program.

This question was approached with the idea that perhaps youth discharged to a structured group setting would be more likely to have achieved educationally and be employed than youth discharged to a family environment. There were several reasons why this might be so. First, many youth discharged to families (whether to a birth, kinship, foster, or adoptive home) were often returning to communities with many distractions and obstacles to working and going to school (Maps 1 to 5 revealed that the neighborhoods in which the families of origin lived were areas with low educational attainment and high unemployment). In contrast the group homes were in more stable

---

2. Not including 21 youths for whom the more stringent self-sufficiency status could not be determined because education or employment information was not known.

Table 13: Discharge Destination From CV for WAY Scholars Who Completed at Least 2.5 Years of the Program (Cohorts 1 to 10)

Discharge Destination	N *	%
Family Environments	**43**	**43%**
Birth/Kinship Home	38	38%
Adoptive Home	1	1%
Foster Home	4	4%
Structured Group Settings	**56**	**56%**
Group Home	51	51%
RTC (Residential Treatment Center)	2	2%
RTF (Residential Treatment Facility)	2	2%
Job Corps	1	1%
Independent Living	1	1%
TOTAL	**100**	**100%**

* Does not include 13 youths living in group homes and 5 in foster homes at the time of recruitment into WAY.

communities, and the professionals associated with such structured group settings had achieved at least a high school education and could serve as employed role models.

Other reasons that structured group setting residents might have done well academically include their regular access to social workers and other social service professionals. Youth had the security of knowing that their basic needs were being met, they had access to educational resources such as computers, and they had constant supervision and one-on-one advocacy through professional staff. In a sense, these staff were to function as "ideal parents," monitoring the academic progress of the youth, setting high expectations for performance, and advocating on the youth's behalf when necessary. These structured group settings were often located in communities with better job opportunities. However, it is important to remember that all WAY scholars, those living with families and those discharged to structured group settings, were assigned WAY Scholarship counselors and received all the benefits of the WAY Scholarship program.

**Table 14: Cross-Tabulation of Discharge Destination by Self-Sufficiency
at the End of the Program for WAY Scholars Cohorts 1 to 10
who Completed at Least 2.5 Years of WAY**

	Family Environment	Group Home and Other	Total
Self-Sufficient	31	51	82
Column %	84%	85%	15%
Not Self-Sufficient	6	9	15
Column %	16%	15%	85%
Total	37	60	97 *

* Twenty-one youths were missing self-sufficiency data.

Table 14 presents the cross-tabulation and chi-square analysis examining the relationship between discharge destination and being on a self-sufficiency trajectory.[3]

As can be seen in Table 14, discharge destination was not statistically associated with self-sufficiency (Chi-square [n=97]=.03, p < .88). Those discharged to family environments and those discharged to structured group settings were equally likely to be self-sufficient at the end of the WAY Scholarship program. Because these findings are counter-intuitive, we decided to look more closely at the data. We were surprised to find that four scholars discharged to a group setting did not complete high school. The case records of those four youth were examined to see if a pattern emerged. On close inspection, it was found that three of the four youths did not stay at the group homes to which they were discharged. Each of these boys had moved several times in the interim and had ended up, by the end of the program, in a family environment.

Thus, it appeared that the place where scholars were initially discharged was not necessarily the residence at which they would spend the majority of their time between discharge from CV and the end of the program. By the end of the program many youths

---

3. For the purposes of these analyses, youth enrolled into WAY from a group home (13 youth) or foster home (5 youth) were coded as being discharged to those places.

had switched living arrangements at least once. Some youths were discharged to family environments that proved to be unsuitable. Conversely, some youths or their parents improved enough to allow a return to family. For other youths, moves to several different group homes occurred before a stable living arrangement was found. For all these reasons, we also chose to look at where youths were living at the end of the program as it related to self-sufficiency. We hypothesized that residence at the end of the 5-year program would better predict self-sufficiency than discharge destination.

Table 15: Cross-Tabulation of the End of Program Residence by Self-Sufficiency for WAY Scholars Cohorts 1 to 10 who Completed at Least 2.5 Years of WAY

	Family Environment	Group Home and Other	Total
Self-Sufficient	34	44	78
Column %	79%	90%	86%
Not Self-Sufficient	9	5	14
Column %	21%	10%	14%
Total	43	49	92 *

* Twenty-one youths were missing self-sufficiency data and an additional five youths were missing end of program residence data.

Table 15 shows that as of the end of the program, 49 of the 92 youths (53%) were living in structured group settings, as compared to 62% (Table 14) at discharge. Some of the youths discharged to group homes were able to return home by the end of the program, and others were either living independently or were in college. Forty-seven percent were living with families at the end of the program, which is slightly higher than the percentage that were living with families at the time of discharge (Table 14). Three were in the military, and one youth was in jail. Table 15 presents a cross-tabulation of self-sufficiency with residence at the end of the program. Chi-square analyses revealed no statistically significant relationship between residence at end of program and self-sufficiency (Chi-square [n=92]=2.04, p < .13).

A methodological issue limits these analyses between residence and self-sufficiency. Neither discharge destination nor residence at the end of the program fully captures the quality or quantity of residences during the approximately four years WAY scholars were in the program and living off CV's campus. Perhaps a more refined measure of residence, one that captures both the number and type of all the different living arrangements WAY youth experienced, would reveal a relationship with self-sufficiency. It is also possible that *stability* in the living arrangement is as important as the setting itself. This is an area for future research.

We also conducted preliminary analyses on the subset of youth who appeared to have spent the majority of their time between CV discharge and end of program in a group home. Of 14 WAY Scholarship youth who spent at least four years in a group home, all but one had received their high school degree by the end of the program. These data are consistent with the strong emphasis in the group homes on education. Yet, we do not know from our data what is cause and what is effect. For example, perhaps youth more likely to drop out of high school are more likely to be expelled from or leave the group homes.

9
■ ■

Findings: Did WAY Scholars Avoid Criminality?

As young adults (between the ages of 22 to 32), how did criminality rates compare for the WAY Scholarship and comparison groups?

◆ For the full sample, there was no statistically significant difference between WAY Scholarship and comparison youth in criminality rates.

◆ Youths who participated in at least 2.5 years of the WAY Scholarship program had marginally significantly lower criminality rates (5%) than youths who did not drop out of the comparison group (15%).

◆ Youths who participated in at least 2.5 years of the WAY Scholarship program had significantly lower criminality rates (5%) than youths who left the program before 2.5 years (35%).

New York State Department of Corrections (DOCS) data regarding prison sentences for youth over the age of 20 were examined for both the WAY scholars and the young men in the comparison group. Youth ranged in age from 22 to 32 at the time the search was conducted (Mean=26.00 years, SD=1.86 years). Variables examined included whether or not a crime was committed, type of crime, length of sentence, and severity of crime.

As can be seen in Table 16, 12 WAY scholars out of 89 (13.5%) in cohorts 1 to 6[1] were sentenced to prison in New York State after reaching the age of 21. Eleven of the 75 youth (14.7%) in the comparison group were sentenced to prison in New York State after reaching the age of 21. This difference was not statistically significant (Chi-square [n=164]=.05, p < .83).[2] A logistic regression was run to control for initial differences

---

1. Cohorts 7 to 10 were excluded from this analysis in part because there was no comparison group and because many youth in the more recent cohorts were not yet 21.

2. These analyses exclude two WAY scholars and one comparison youth who died before turning 21. In

Table 16: Cross-Tabulation of Incarceration History: WAY Versus Comparison Group (Cohorts 1 to 6)

	WAY	Comparison	Total
NO PRISON HISTORY	77	64	141
Column %	86.5%	85.3%	86.0%
PRISON HISTORY	12	11	23
Column %	13.5%	14.7%	14.0%
Total	89	75	164

between these two groups (whether youngsters had a history of being neglected or abandoned and whether they had been in foster care placement prior to admission to the RTC); these did not alter the results of these analyses.

The crimes for which youth were charged include robbery, assault, rape, possession of a controlled substance, sale of a controlled substance, weapons possession, burglary, criminal contempt, and criminal mischief. About 26% of the crimes (6 out of 23) were categorized as being economic and nonviolent in nature (burglary or the sale of a controlled substance) and 74% (17 out of 23) were violent (robbery, assault, rape, and so forth). A cross-tabulation revealed that the WAY and comparison groups did not differ in the proportion of economic and violent crimes committed (Chi-square [n=23]=1.16, $p < .38$).

The average minimum sentence was 3.2 years. There were no statistically significant difference between WAY (Mean=3.9, SD=3.7) and comparison group youth (Mean=2.4, SD=1.7) in length of minimum sentence (t [21]=1.2, $p < .24$]. Severity of crimes was also examined with the DOCS five-point scale (one is more severe and five is less severe). The average severity for all crimes was 3.4 (SD=.98). There was a trend for

---

addition, two WAY youth (one of whom completed more than 2.5 years of the program) were excluded from these analyses because they were sentenced for a crime committed under age 21 but are still serving out their sentences. Five other youth (three comparison group and two scholars), also sentenced for a crime committed under age 21 were later readmitted after turning 21 (generally because of parole violations).

WAY youth (Mean=3.0, SD=1.0) to commit more serious crimes than the comparison group (Mean=3.7, SD=.8) (t [21]=1.9, p < .08).

When only those who completed at least half of the 5-year WAY Scholarship program (71% of those enrolled) were compared with those who did not drop out of the comparison group (80% of those enrolled), the results look quite different. WAY scholars had lower criminality rates (5%) than the comparison group (15%). As seen in Table 17, only 3 of these WAY Scholarship youth were sentenced after turning 21, versus 9 comparison youth. This difference between the groups is marginally statistically significant using a one-tailed test (Chi-square [n=124]=3.54, p < .06). Consequently, among those who stayed with the WAY Scholarship program or did not drop out of the comparison group, WAY Scholarship status was associated with lower criminality rates than the comparison group status.

A series of logistic regressions was conducted to controll for initial differences.[3] These logistic regressions did not alter the results. In each case, program participation was associated with lower rates of criminality, over and above initial group differences.[4] Consequently, among those who stayed with the WAY Scholarship program for at least 2.5 years or remained in contact with CV from the comparison group, program participation was associated with lower criminality rates. Because of the low incidence of criminality among the nondropouts (n=3), it was not possible to compare the groups on length of sentence, severity of crime, or type of crime.

A further analysis examined whether WAY Scholarship youth who stayed in the program for at least 2.5 years fared better on adult criminality than youth who dropped out of the program (Table 18). Data from the New York State DOCS revealed that scholars who remained active in the program for at least 2.5 years were less likely to be imprisoned after the age of 21 than youth who were dropouts. Whereas only 3 of 63 scholars (5%) active for at least half of the 5-year program were sentenced after the age of 21,[5] 9 of the

---

3. Because of too much pair-wise missing data, five regressions were conducted entering each of the five background variables as the first step and the group variable (WAY or comparison) as the second step.
4. The entire model, entering the variable for which the groups differed as the first step and group (WAY or comparison) as the second step, was statistically significant for four of the five variables. For the fifth variable (the amount of time youth spent at CV after enrollment in WAY), for which there was substantial missing data because group and foster home youth needed to be excluded from the analysis, the model was significant at the level of a trend (p < .08).
5. This excludes two youth who died before turning 21 and one youth who was sentenced before turning 21.

Table 17: Cross-Tabulation of Incarceration History: WAY > 2.5 Years Versus Comparison Nondropouts (Cohorts 1 to 6)

	WAY > 2.5 Years	Comparison Nondropouts	Total
NO PRISON HISTORY	60	52	112
Column %	95.2%	85.2%	90.3%
PRISON HISTORY	3	9	12
Column %	4.8%	14.8%	9.7%
Total	63	61	124

Table 18: Cross-Tabulation of Incarceration History: WAY > 2.5 Years Versus WAY Dropouts (Cohorts 1 to 6)

	WAY > 2.5 Years	WAY Dropouts	Total
NO PRISON HISTORY	60	17	77
Column %	95.2%	65.4%	86.5%
PRISON HISTORY	3	9	12
Column %	4.8%	34.6%	13.5%
Total	63	26	89

26 (35%) who left the program before completing 2.5 years received prison sentences after the age of 21.[6] This relationship is statistically significant (Chi-square $[n=89]=14.06$, $p<.01$). Thus, staying with the program was associated with lower rates of criminality.

In order to determine whether preexisting differences between the two groups accounted for subsequent differences in criminality rates, a logistic regression was conducted. Variables on which the two groups differed[7] at admission to CV were entered as a first block, and group (dropout or participator for at least 2.5 years) as the second step. Results revealed that the group comparison was still significant even after controlling for initial group differences. Thus, these initial differences did not account for differential rates of criminality.

Exploratory analyses were then conducted to determine whether the youths who dropped out of WAY Scholarship were initially more prone to criminal behavior. In these analyses, we focused on 10 of the preadmission problem behaviors that could be considered pre-delinquent.[8] A summary score was created for each youth of the number (out of 10) of problem behaviors exhibited prior to admission to CV. These 10 behaviors were taken from the list of 14 problem behaviors (Table 3). The analyses with the summary score of the 10 behaviors did not reveal statistically significant differences. Youths who remained involved in WAY Scholarship for at least 2.5 years exhibited on average just under two (Mean=1.8, SD=1.4) behaviors, while youths who dropped out exhibited on average just over two (Mean=2.2, SD=1.3). This difference was not statistically significantly different (t $[127]=1.37$, $p < .18$]. These data suggest that the dropout group was not more prone to criminal behavior prior to the WAY Scholarship program. Perhaps dropping out of the program set them on a more negative path. Future research could examine this process more closely.

---

6. One youth sentenced before turning 21 was excluded from this analysis. Two of these nine youth were sentenced before turning 21 but returned for violating parole after turning 21. (The relationship between participating in at least 2.5 years and criminality was statistically significant even when these two youth were excluded from the analysis.)

7. Analyses comparing WAY cohorts 1 to 6 dropouts with WAY cohorts 1 to 6 youth who participated at least 2.5 years on the 27 background variables revealed two statistically significant differences: dropouts were less likely to have a history of being physically abused (p. < .05), and dropouts stayed on the campus of the RTC for a shorter period of time after enrollment in the program (p. < .06).

8. Cohorts 1 to 10 were used in these analyses to increase the sample size.

How did criminality rates for WAY scholars compare to national rates?

Criminality rates were about 14% for WAY Scholarship youth as a group, 5% for participants who remained in the program for at least 2.5 years, and 35% for dropouts who left before the halfway point. The criminality rate for the comparison group was also around 14%. The question naturally arose as to whether the rate of 5% for the WAY scholars who participated for at least 2.5 years was better than rates for other high-risk groups who did not receive an intervention. Yet, identifying exact comparisons was not possible because of the variation in how criminality is measured across studies. Some researchers focus on arrest rates, while others assess rates of convictions for certain types of crimes (i.e., felonies as opposed to misdemeanors). Variation in age at time of criminal behavior also occurred.

Despite this lack of exact comparisons, national data show that between 50% and 60% of the general population of men will be arrested in their lifetime (McDonald et al. 1996). Studies of former foster care youth have reported that 14% to 22% spent time in jail, a figure well above the 5% for the WAY Scholarship youth who participated in at least 2.5 years of the program (McDonald et al. 1996). The Vera Institute of Justice's Project Confirm reported on its website that foster care youth are overrepresented in the New York City detention system. A CWLA (1997) study found that 50% of the 66 9- to 12-year-olds arrested in one county in California were foster care youth, even though such youth represented less than 2% of the general population. Taken together, these data suggest that the 5% rate of adult convictions among the WAY scholars who participated in more than 2.5 years of the program was below the expected rate for youth in the foster care system. The 14% rate for the comparison group and for the program youth as a whole also is probably lower than expected, although in the absence of exact comparisons this is hard to confirm. If these rates are in fact lower than expected, CV may have been a contributing factor to improved outcomes for all youth (regardless of participation in WAY Scholarship). That all CV youth were removed from their negative environments and received intensive mental health services from CV functions as a confounding variable and highlights the fact that the effect of residential treatment per se is an understudied area.

10

Findings: How Did Youths Feel About Their Counselor, and Was "Mentoring" Associated with Positive Outcomes?

Did WAY scholars experience their counselors as helpful mentors?

♦ Three-fourths of WAY scholars interviewed spontaneously reported positive feelings about their counselors, indicating that they played an instrumental role in helping them make the transition from CV to life in the community.

Interviews with 39 former WAY scholars in 1997 from cohorts 1 to 6 produced many comments about their relationships with their WAY counselors (36 of the interviews rendered codable transcripts). The vast majority of these scholars (n=27, 75%) spontaneously reported very positive feelings about their counselors, indicating that they were instrumental in helping them make the transition from CV to life with their biological family, a foster family, or in a group home.

Many youths felt close to their counselors and experienced as helpful and meaningful the ongoing involvement. Former scholars reported receiving both concrete support as well as emotional support.

★ *My counselor had a way of working miracles.*

★ *My [first] counselor was my first best friend that I ever had. [My second counselor] took me on interviews on her own personal time. I remember we would be coming back from colleges at 11:00 at night. To me that's going beyond the call of duty. She went out of her way to help me.*

★ *I think the most significant thing that the WAY program has offered me is the idea that that there is this person in your corner whose total role is to be there to support you during the most crucial times.*

★ *He brought it to me like this; whatever you need we can do it for you. They was [sic] always there telling me what was important. How to stay in school and, you know, keep it going. They showed me a sense of responsibility.*

★ *My goals were nurtured. They motivated me when my WAY counselors spoke with me.*

★ *He was my father. [The counselor] was very on my back, very concerned. He was a very supportive man and has been in my corner. There were times when I got into some heavy things and he would come out and visit me. It is guys like [him] that makes this program happen.*

★ *He sat me down and we talked about where I wanted to be within the next 20 years, and I told him I wanted to go to college and I wanted to deal with computers. He instilled in me that if I put my mind to something that I can do it.*

★ *They help you find a job and they help you get group home placements.*

Youth reported that their counselors were persistent in making the effort to keep in touch after the youth were discharged from CV.

★ *Yes, he stayed in touch with me. Actually, he was quite annoying because he always wanted to meet with me at 6:30 to 7:00 in the morning.*

★ *They always kept in touch.*

★ *My old counselor, he used to come out and visit my family and talk with them.*

★ *I like people checking up on me even though I am not there [at CV] anymore.*

★ *My counselors visited me and made sure I was okay.*

★ *He would come up to my school or wherever I worked at. I mean he always used to call and check up on me. "Are you all right? Do you need anything?" They always came through. The WAY Scholarship was always there for me.*

★   *When you leave it's like they are not finished with you until they still got their arms around you.*

Counselors were perceived as available to help when called upon.

★   *If I did need anything the counselor was there.*

★   *He was there; he was always around. He was always involved with whatever I did.*

★   *They never stopped seeing me because of the trips I kept making back up here [to CV] to let everyone know I'm doing fine or let everyone know I need help, someone to talk to. As much as I kept coming back for more and more help, I still felt I was always a part of it.*

Some youth became so attached to their counselors that they became upset when the counselors left the program.

★   *When he left it was a tremendous blow to me. Not only did he leave, he left for upstate so he was going to be a distance away where I knew I wasn't going to have the same relationship.*

★   *He informed me I was going to get another counselor. I didn't want that; it bothered me. For a while I was really mad. I just felt betrayed. I didn't want to get to know another counselor.*

Many of the young men expressed the idea that they could have benefited from the ongoing support and guidance of the counselor beyond the 5-year program.

★   *I think if I had someone like [WAY counselors] they would have told me to calm down, don't take 18 credits in college. I am sure they would have put balance in my life. That's the thing I was lacking.*

★   *The low point is when you realize you are on your own. Nobody is there to support you. Nobody is there to push you.*

★   *I would have liked to [have a counselor in college]. The first year of college was unbelievable. It probably would have changed my decision to transfer.*

★   *There is nobody on your back telling you to save. You have to do it on your own.*

Five of the interviewees had no specific memory of their WAY counselor; three others remembered their WAY counselor but did not feel that the contact had been productive or positive.

★ *Nobody ever contacted me.*

★ *I wanted [my counselor] to help me out. I wanted a lot of people to help me. They didn't care about me.*

★ *The counselor wasn't working very closely with me. In those years I did feel alone. I remember feeling like I was in this all by myself. It was a very tough thing to go through.*

One young man had positive feelings toward one of his counselors but thought very poorly of another counselor.

★ *I didn't like him a lot. I couldn't stand him. He was a liar, a fraud, and he wasn't into people. He was just there for the money. He promised to help me when I left CV, [but] he didn't do anything of the sort.*

In all, the remembrances of interviewed former WAY scholars about their counselors were positive. Three-quarters of the youth had positive feelings toward their counselors. Even after 10 years, they remembered the relationship with strong feelings. Many felt that the counselor was a critically important person in their journey toward adulthood, providing concrete support and assistance as well as emotional support and nurturance.

Was the match between counselors and youth or the stability of the relationship associated with positive outcomes?

The following list pertains to WAY youth in cohorts 6 to 10:

♦ Most youth worked with counselors of the same gender and same ethnicity for the majority of their involvement in WAY Scholarship.

♦ Scholars averaged 2.5 switches in assigned counselors over the course of their involvement in WAY.

♦ The average time a youth worked with one counselor was over 3 years.

◆ Higher proportions of gender matches between scholars and counselors were associated with greater end-of-program self-sufficiency and educational attainment; fewer counselor switches were associated with greater self-sufficiency and greater educational attainment; longer counselor relationships were associated with educational attainment.

Data were available on the youth-counselor relationship for all scholars in cohorts 6 to 10. Four variables were examined: (1) whether a youth worked with a female counselor, (2) percentage of time in the program that youth worked with a counselor of the same ethnicity, (3) number of counselor switches, and (4) length of time with one counselor (for the relationship that lasted the longest time). Tables 19 through 22 present the frequency distributions of these four variables.

As can be seen in Tables 19 and 20, most scholars worked with counselors of the same gender and same ethnicity for the majority of their involvement in the program. Only one youth was paired exclusively with female counselors, and 36 of the youth (46.8%) worked only with male counselors. Thus, most boys were paired with a male counselor most of the time. In fact, the mean for gender matches was almost 92%. Turning to ethnicity matches between youth and their WAY counselors, the data are somewhat more varied. The mean of 49.58% indicates that scholars were matched with counselors of the same ethnicity about half the time in the program. Thirteen of the 72 boys (18%) matched their counselor's ethnicity their whole time in the program. Forty-three scholars (60%) experienced a range of ethnic matches over the course of their involvement in WAY Scholarship, and 16 (22%) boys never shared the same ethnicity with a counselor for any portion of their involvement in the program. A closer look revealed that all 16 of these boys were from Latino backgrounds and that during their involvement in WAY Scholarship there were only two Latino counselors (one on staff for 3 years and one on staff for only 6 months). Thus, providing an ethnic match for Latino youth was a challenge for the WAY Scholarship program during these years.

Table 19: Percentage of Time Youth Assigned to Counselor of the Same Gender (Cohorts 6 to 10)

Percent of Time With a Match	N	%
0 to 50	3	3.9%
70 to 79	8	10.4%
80 to 89	5	6.5%
90 to 99	25	32.4%
100	36	46.8%
TOTAL	*77*	*100%*

Mean = 91.80%, SD = 16.02%

Table 20: Percentage of Time Youth Assigned to Counselor of the Same Ethnicity (Cohorts 6 to 10)

Percent of Time With a Match	N	%
0	16	22.2%
1 to 19	9	12.5%
20 to 39	8	11.1%
40 to 59	5	
60 to 79	9	12.5%
80 to 99	12	16.7%
100	13	18.1%
TOTAL	*72*	*100%*

Mean = 49.58%, SD = 40.23%

Tables 21 and 22 present data regarding counselor stability.

Table 21: Number of Switches in Counselors for WAY Scholars (Cohorts 6 to 10)

Number of Switches	N	%
0	12	15.6%
1	14	18.2%
2	19	24.7%
3	10	13.0%
4	11	14.3%
5	8	10.4%
6	1	1.3%
7	1	1.3%
8	1	1.3%
TOTAL	*77*	*100%*

Mean = 2.43%, SD = 1.82%

Table 22: Longest Working Relationship with a Counselor for WAY Scholars (Cohorts 6 to 10)

Months	N	%
1 to 20	14	18.2%
21 to 30	16	20.8%
31 to 40	19	24.7%
41 to 50	18	23.4%
51 to 60	10	13.0%
TOTAL	*77*	*100%*

Mean = 34.10%, SD = 14.37%

As can be seen from these two tables, although most boys were assigned more than one counselor over the course of WAY, most also experienced at least one long-term counselor relationship. Scholars averaged 2.5 switches in WAY counselors over the course of their involvement in WAY Scholarship. Twelve scholars experienced no switches, working with only one counselor. Fourteen scholars experienced only one switch, indicating that they worked with two counselors. Nineteen boys experienced two switches, indicating that they worked with three counselors or were reassigned to an earlier counselor. Twenty-nine boys experienced three to five switches, and three boys experienced six to eight switches. A switch was due either to staff turnover and/or to planned counselor changes based on staff judgments of youth needs. The mean of the longest counselor relationship was 34.10 months, just under 3 years.

Next, each of these four counselor variables was correlated with employment, education, savings, and self-sufficiency in order to ascertain whether counselor match and stability were associated with positive outcomes. The outcomes examined were the proportion of time working, total savings, educational success at end of program, and whether a youth was on a self-sufficiency trajectory at the end of the 5-year program. These four outcomes were chosen because cohorts 6 to 10 had data on both the four counselor variables and these outcomes, allowing for correlational analyses to be conducted.

Of these 16 correlations, 2 (12.5%) were significant and another 3 (19%) were marginally significant (Table 23). Working only with male counselors was associated with greater self-sufficiency (R=.39, p < .01) and a trend for greater likelihood of educational success at the end of the program (R=.25, p < .07). Fewer counselor switches were associated with greater self-sufficiency (R=-.41, p < .01) and greater likelihood of educational success at the end of the program (R=-.26, p < .06). The duration of the longest youth-counselor relationship tended to be associated with educational status at the end of the program (R=.25, p < .07). Looking at the data by outcome, it can be seen that 3 counselor variables were associated with education at the end of the program (gender match, number of counselor switches, and length of relationship). Two variables were associated with self-sufficiency trajectory at the end of the program (gender match and number of switches). No counselor variables were associated with the percentage of time working in the program or with savings. Thus, these data partly confirm the two overarching hypotheses, that counselor stability (fewer switches and length of relationship) and counselor similarity (gender and ethnicity matches) would be associated with positive program outcomes.

Table 23: Correlations of Counselor Variables with Employment and End of Program Outcome Variables (valid n in parentheses)

	All Counselors Male?	Percentage of Same Race and Ethnicity Pairings	Number of Counselor Switches	Length of Longest Counselor Relationship
Percent of Time Working in Program	—	—	—	—
Total Savings	—	—	—	—
Education at End of Program	.25+ (55)	—	-.26+ (55)	.25+ (55)
Self-Sufficient at End of Program	.39** (52)	—	-.41* (52)	—

+ = p < .10
* = p < .05
** = p < .01

11 ■ ■■■■■■■■■■■■■■■■■■■■■■■■■■■ ■

Discussion

Directions for Future Research

These data represent the results of 15 years of studying the WAY Scholarship program. Considerable effort has been put into designing the study; recruiting the program participants; developing the comparison group; following up on the youth; and collecting, analyzing, and interpreting the data. While this report reflects that effort, much has been learned over the years about conducting applied, longitudinal research in a child welfare setting. If we were starting over today, there are many things we would do differently based on our extensive experience working with this population.

♦ Locating former foster care youth was extremely difficult. Better processes could have been built into the study from the beginning to allow for longer-term follow-up. Keeping in touch every year would have allowed for updated address information rather than trying to find youth after years had passed. Incentives could have been built into the research process and budget for keeping in contact with everyone who was enrolled in the study. Obtaining the names and addresses of several contact persons who would have known youth whereabouts also might have helped.

♦ Collecting sociodemographic background data from agency records (some of it over 10 years old) created problems for the study. Some records could not be found or were lost in the fire. Other records contained ambiguities that could have been clarified if the data had been collected at the time youth entered the study rather than several years afterward. We believe that background data should be collected *prospectively* from the youth, from their caseworkers, and from available documentation rather than from agency records several years after youth are discharged from care.

◆ Much of the educational and employment data were self-reported. More rigorous methodologies could have been employed to verify and confirm this information. For example, incentives could be offered for youth to provide documentation (e.g., pay stubs, high school diplomas), and random checks of the veracity of data could have been conducted in order to strengthen confidence in the findings. Further, obtaining employment outcome data on the full sample (rather than just the youth who agreed to be interviewed and who had participated for at least 2.5 years) would increase the generalizability of these important outcome findings.

◆ Educational data on the full sample would have allowed for more rigorous analyses of differences between the WAY Scholarship and comparison youth, an important outcome of the study. Yet, the youth considered dropouts of the WAY Scholarship and comparison groups were not incorporated into the initial follow-up components of the study. Only several years later was it decided that including them would enhance the credibility of the design; at that point, it was not possible to locate them for long-term outcome data collection.

◆ It is clear from our analyses that youth tended to move several times in the years following discharge from CV. We believe that moving was a potentially important variable for understanding outcomes, yet we had insufficient data to carefully examine its effect. What is needed is a thorough assessment of all residences youth have had between the time of discharge from care and the end of the program in order to ascertain the effects of the number and quality of these environments on relevant outcomes.

◆ The youth who dropped out of WAY Scholarship are understudied. Although only one-fourth of the total group, they represent an important subset because they appear to have worse criminality outcomes. Educational and employment data on these youth would have shed light on a fuller range of outcomes. Future research should include interviews with the program dropouts and their counselors to try to ascertain why dropping out of the WAY Scholarship program was associated with higher rates of adult criminality. These interviews could perhaps help identify what could have been done to maintain their involvement in the program. Perhaps profiles of youth most likely to drop out could be created and used to target them with more intensive services.

♦ The youth-counselor relationship also warrants more careful attention. Our data suggest that certain aspects of the relationship were associated with somewhat better outcomes, although the correlations were modest. Future research should take a much closer look at what aspects of the counselor relationship are associated with positive outcomes for scholars. For example, determining whether a counselor switch was planned by the program or due to staff turnover could lead to a better understanding of the role of counselor changes on outcomes. A particularly fruitful area of inquiry is the quality of the relationship between the youth and counselor from the perspectives of both parties.

♦ The qualitative interviews with the WAY scholars as adults proved to be extremely interesting windows into their lives and to what the WAY Scholarship program meant to them. Future research should also include interviews with the counselors to hear their ideas about the challenges and triumphs of being a WAY counselor and what they need to be more effective in their roles. Determining which factors were associated with counselor turnover could also make a contribution to improving WAY Scholarship and similar programs.

♦ Future research should measure in depth the level of involvement (from the perspectives of youth and staff) in different aspects of the program in order to more reliably measure program participation and program attrition. The validity of the 2.5 year cut-off needs to be determined. Perhaps there are other ways to measure participation. The philosophy of the WAY Scholarship program was grounded in the belief that the counselor would function as a surrogate parent, ever available, even in the face of apparent rejection on the part of the youth. Thus, periodic absence was viewed as part of normal adolescent demonstrations of independence rather than an act of dropping out of the program. The low numbers of youth considered dropouts is partly based on the fact that counselors were reluctant to give up on a youth no matter how disinterested in the program he might have appeared. Objective data regarding level of participation would have complemented these staff judgments.

Lessons Learned and Recommendations for Practice

Youth Discharged From Foster Care Need Intensive Aftercare Services

Youth discharged from foster care are still quite vulnerable, with long-standing family and school difficulties. Many flounder as they make the transition to a less restrictive placement or back home. They need support and guidance to sustain the gains they have made while in care. High reentry rates bear this out. For example, Festinger (1996) found that one-fifth of all discharges from foster care resulted in reentry within two years. Even youth who age out of foster care evidence academic, emotional, and behavioral problems. For example, Blome (1997) found that former foster care youth were more likely to exhibit emotional and behavioral problems than a comparison group. Courtney and Piliavin (1998) also found that youth experienced many practical and emotional problems once discharged from care. The young men who participated in the WAY Scholarship program were no exception. Discharge from care did not represent an end to their mental health, educational, and/or social support needs. They experienced many financial and emotional hardships in the years following discharge.

In New York, residential treatment costs roughly $50,000 per year, and the average length of stay is 2 years. For youth who are discharged to their own responsibility, the length of stay is generally much longer. Funding for aftercare in most states, including New York, is nonexistent. Aftercare services, such as those provided by WAY Scholarship, costs roughly $3,000 per youth per year—hardly a steep investment to sustain the gains made during years in expensive out-of-home care. *It is recommended that long-term aftercare services, available for years not months, be provided for adolescents discharged from RTCs.*

Aftercare Services Should Follow Youth Across Service Systems

High-risk youth in general, and young people discharged from foster care in particular, tend to move frequently—among and between relatives and friends and in and out of different service systems. Cook's (1994) follow-up study of youth discharged from care revealed that one-third of youth moved five or more times in the two to four years following discharge. This was certainly true of the WAY Scholarship participants. No matter where the youth were headed to—group home, biological family, foster family, Job Corps, or more restrictive level of care—most relocated several times in the years following discharge. Some WAY Scholarship youth moved from the supervision of CV to the care of another agency, while others moved in and out of foster care several times in the ensuing years.

Private funding for the program allowed the WAY Scholarship counselors to follow the youth and provide services, regardless of what other system youth entered. This approach stands in stark contrast to the traditional community-based approach in which youth are expected to start over with each relocation or involvement in a new service system. Many adolescents are reluctant to form new relationships so we need to nurture the good relationships that have been established and allow adults to stay with the youth. In that way, no matter what community youth move to, no matter what system they are in, a trusted adult can provide the continuity that links youth to the services they need. *It is recommended that aftercare staff be given flexibility in funding and in access to youth to provide continuity in care.*

Youth Leaving Care Need Long-Term Counseling and Mentoring

The idea of offering 5 years of intensive aftercare services to foster care youth was unheard of 15 years ago, when the WAY Scholarship program was developed. It still is. Yet, interviews with the WAY scholars revealed that, for many, 5 years was not enough. Most could have benefited from an even longer-term commitment from the program, one that extended well into their young adulthood. This was true for youth in college who yearned for adult guidance and support as they navigated a new and demanding world. It was true for youth in the working world striving to become responsible adults. It was also true for youth still struggling to overcome a lifetime of family trauma and not yet on a path of self-sufficiency. For many youth, the WAY Scholarship counselor was the most important adult in their lives. For them, the end of the program came too soon. *It is recommended that aftercare services be provided to former foster care youth on a long-term basis, well into their young adulthood.*

Mentors Should be Paid Professionals

Mentors for this population should be paid professionals with reasonable caseloads (15 to 20 youth) and clearly defined expectations and measures of accountability. Youth need to feel that at least one person has a strong stake and interest in their success. For some youth leaving residential treatment, a loving, supportive family member awaits them. Even in these circumstances, the involvement of a mentor is usually welcomed and needed. For the majority of older youth in residential care, there is no one. These young people are often discharged to their own responsibility. The paid professional mentors in the WAY Scholarship program were there to provide them with support, guidance, and caring along the way from discharge through young adulthood.

The current focus on volunteer mentors for at-risk youth that is sweeping the country is extremely positive, and it is important for many vulnerable youngsters. But for youth discharged from residential treatment, it is probably not enough. Volunteers cannot be expected to go to the extreme lengths that many of the WAY Scholarship counselors had to go to in order to develop and sustain relationships with the program participants. Volunteers cannot be held accountable the same way paid mentors can, and they cannot be expected to be versed in the range of issues and systems relevant to the lives of WAY Scholarship youth. For example, WAY counselors helped youth access housing and mental health services, detected early warning signs of drug use, advocated within the public school system, provided guidance in completing college applications and applications for financial assistance, and so forth. The needs of the youth are too great and the demands on the counselor too many for anyone other than a paid professional to reasonably be expected to do this kind of work, day in and day out, year in and year out. *It is recommended that mentors in programs like WAY be paid professionals who have the time and skills necessary to make a difference in the lives of young people.*

Programmatic Challenges

Youth Need Help Preparing for a Career

Young adults not bound for college need the most help in planning for their future, yet they receive the least assistance and face the greatest risks in the job market (Orfield & Paul 1994). This is partly because high school general education alone does not provide adequate preparation for a successful career, and no real guidance system is in place in American high schools for noncollege-bound youth (Mendel 1995). Nationwide, a 1994 survey found that only one-fourth of school guidance counselors spent any real time helping students with career planning. A high school degree is not a guarantee of achieving a stable employment history at a job with a livable wage. Thus, it is no surprise that one-third of all youth with a high school education fail to find stable employment by the time they reach age 30 (Osterman 1991, cited in Mendel 1995).

Not all WAY Scholarship youth attended college. The employment histories of the youth interviewed revealed that many went from job to job without actually developing a career path that would ultimately lead to a satisfying and well-paying livelihood. Although some obtained full-time employment with decent wages and health benefits, many had not. They were what the U.S. Department of Labor (1999) refers to as "the stuck, not the skilled." *Thus, a challenge for the WAY Scholarship and similar programs is to help noncollege-bound participants develop career paths that will result in jobs that pay a livable wage.*

Youth Need Help Succeeding in College

The 20 highest paying professions in this country require at least a bachelor's degree. College graduates on average earn 71% more than high school graduates (U.S. Department of Labor 1999). Attending college is not enough. Graduation is critical. WAY scholars appeared to understand the importance of pursuing postsecondary education. Fully one-fourth of WAY scholars at the end of the program and 40% at age 21 had participated in some postsecondary education. Yet, one of the themes that emerged in the interviews with the WAY Scholarship participants was that not all youth enrolled in college graduated.[1] It is important to remember that WAY scholars are not screened into the program based on academic success. To the contrary, all WAY Scholarship youth were classified as requiring special education and many were years behind in their education at the time of enrollment into WAY.

For most WAY Scholarship participants who attended college, postsecondary education was much harder than they had anticipated, both academically and socially. For many, the start of college overlapped with their "graduation" from the WAY program—either because the youth moved away to attend college or because it coincided with their fifth year in the program. Unfortunately, entering college did not signify that these young men no longer needed the support of their WAY counselors. Quite the opposite was true; many spoke of feeling overwhelmed by the academic demands of their coursework and by the array of choices they had to make on their own. They had to decide which courses to take, how many courses to take each semester, and they had to learn how to balance social and athletic interests with schoolwork. College is a demanding time for any young person, filled with many new experiences and challenges, a time when adult support and guidance are needed.

An additional challenge for the WAY scholars was that, although they were accepted into college, some were not prepared academically to meet the demands of their coursework. They did not have the study skills and discipline nor the foundation of a solid academic high school education to succeed in college (many had achieved GEDs, spe-

---

1. Data are not yet available on college graduation rates of WAY scholars.

cial education degrees, or had suffered academically after attending many different high schools). Moreover, many WAY youth in college did not have a home to visit during holidays and other school breaks. Youth over the age of 21 were no longer eligible for services from CV even though they had no other "home." Thus, in addition to the academic stresses WAY scholars faced, holidays and vacations posed both logistical and emotional challenges for these youth. Some stayed temporarily at their former group homes or came "home" to CV for the holidays. *Thus, a challenge for the WAY program is to determine how best to prepare these young men for a successful college experience. What kinds of supports and assistance do they need so that they can not only attend college but also become college graduates? Many WAY youth are on the path towards success, but even they are in need of continued support as they enter adulthood.*

References

American Youth Policy Forum. (1997). *Some things do make a difference for youth.* Washington, DC: Institute for Educational Leadership.

Anderson, E. (1997). Violence and the inner-city street code. In J. McCord (Ed.), *Violence and childhood in the inner city.* New York: Cambridge University Press.

Baker, A.J.L. (1997a). Improving parent involvement programs and practice: A qualitative study of parent perceptions. *School Community Journal, 7*(1), 9–36.

Baker, A.J.L. (1997b). Improving parent involvement programs and practice: A qualitative study of teacher perceptions. *School Community Journal, 7*(2), 27–66.

Blome, W. (1997). What happens to foster kids: Educational experiences of a random sample of foster care youth and a matched group of non-foster care youth. *Child and Adolescent Social Work Journal, 14,* 41–53.

Burnett, G. (1992). Career Academies: Educating urban students for career success. *ERIC Digest,* number 84. ERIC Clearinghouse on Urban Education. New York: Columbia University.

Catterall, J.S. (1987). An intensive group counseling dropout prevention intervention: Some cautions on isolating at-risk adolescents within high schools. *American Educational Research Journal, 24,* 521–540.

Center for Human Resources. (1993). *Practitioner's guide to program options/drop out prevention strategies for in-school youth.* Waltham, MA: Brandeis University.

Chapman, W., & Katz, M. (1981). *Survey of career information systems in secondary schools.* Princeton: Educational Testing Service.

Child Welfare League of America. (1997). *Sacramento County community intervention program: Findings from a comprehensive study of community partners in child welfare, law enforcement, juvenile justice, and the Child Welfare League of America.* Washington, DC: Author.

Citizens' Committee for the Children of New York. (1997). *Keeping track of New York City's children.* New York: Author.

Cook, R. (1988). Trends and needs in programming for independent living. *Child Welfare, 67,* 497–514.

Cook, R. (1994). Are we helping foster care youth prepare for their future? *Children and Youth Services Review, 16,* 213–229.

Courtney, M., & Piliavin, I. (1998). *Foster youth transition to adulthood: Outcomes 12 to 18 months after leaving out-of-home care.* Unpublished manuscript.

Epstein, J. (1995, May). School/family/community partnerships: Caring for the children we share. *Phi Delta Kappan,* 703–713.

Evans, B. (1997). *Youth in foster care.* New York: Garland Publishing.

Fanshel, D. (1992). Foster care as a two-tiered system. *Children and Youth Services Review, 14,* 49–60.

Farkas, G., Olsen, Stromsdorfer, E., Sharpe, L., Skidmore, F., Smith, D., & Merrill, S. (1984). *Post-program impacts of the Youth Incentive Entitlement Pilot Projects.* Washington, DC: Manpower Demonstration Research Corporation.

Farrell, E. (1990). *Hanging in and dropping out: Voices of at-risk high school students.* New York: Teachers College Press.

Federal Interagency Forum on Child and Family Statistics. (1999). *America's children: Key national indicators of wellbeing.* Washington DC: Author.

Ferguson, R.F., & Clay, P.L. (1996). *YouthBuild in developmental perspective: A formative evaluation of the Youthbuild demonstration project.* Cambridge: Massachusetts Institute of Technology.

Festinger, T. (1983). *No one ever asked us...A postscript to foster care.* New York: Columbia University Press.

Festinger, T. (1996). Going home and returning to foster care. *Children and Youth Services Report, 18,* 383–402.

Fletcher, B.J. (1997). Same-race practice: Do we expect too much or too little? *Child Welfare, 76,* 213–237.

Grossman, J.B. (Ed.). (1999). *Contemporary Issues in Mentoring.* Philadelphia: Public/Private Ventures.

Grossman, J.B., & Garry, E.M. (1997). *Mentoring—A proven delinquency-prevention strategy. Juvenile Justice Bulletin.* Washington DC: Office of Juvenile Justice and Delinquency Prevention.

Hahn, A. (1994). *Evaluation of the Quantum Opportunities Program: Did the program work?* Waltham, MA: Brandies University.

Harlow, C.W. (1998). *Profile of Jail Inmates 1996.* Washington, DC: U.S. Department of Justice.

Holzer, H. (1996). *What employers want: Job prospects for less-educated workers.* New York: Russell Sage Foundation.

Imel, S. (1993). Vocational education's role in dropout prevention. *ERIC Digest.* ED355455. Washington, DC: ERIC Clearinghouse on Tests, Measurement, and Evaluation.

Kazis, R. (1993). *Improving the transition from school to work in the United States.* Washington, DC: American Youth Policy Forum.

Kazis, R., & Kopp, H. (1997). *Both sides now: New directions in promoting work and learning for disadvantaged youth. A report to the Annie E. Casey Foundation.* Boston: Jobs for the Future.

Kennedy, R. (1992). *Race, crime, and the law.* New York: Pantheon Books.

Kurdek, L., Fine, M., & Sinclair, R. (1995, April). School adjustment in sixth graders: Parenting transitions, family climate, and peer norm effects. *Child Development, 66,* 430–445.

Levin, H.M. (1983). Youth unemployment and its educational consequences. *Educational Evaluation and Policy Analysis, 5,* 231–247.

Luster, T., & McAdoo, P. (1994). Factors related to the achievement and adjustment of young African-American children. *Child Development, 65,* 1080–1094.

Mallon, G. (1998). After care, then where? Outcomes of an independent living program. *Child Welfare, 77,* 61–79.

Manpower Demonstration Research Corporation. (1983). *Findings on youth employment: Lessons from MDRC research.* New York: Author.

Massey, D.S., & Denton, N.A. (1993). *American apartheid: Segregation and the making of the underclass.* Cambridge: Harvard University Press.

Mauer, M. (1990). *Young black Americans and the criminal justice system: A growing national problem.* Washington, DC: The Sentencing Project.

Mauer, M., & Huling, T. (1995). *Young black Americans and the criminal justice system: Five years later.* Washington, DC: The Sentencing Project.

McDonald, T.P., Allen, R.I., Westerfelt, A., & Piliavin, I. (1996). *Assessing the long-term effects of foster care.* Washington, DC: Child Welfare League of America.

McMillen, M.M., Kaufman, P., Hausken, E.G., & Bradby, D. (1993). *Dropout rates in the United States: 1992.* Washington, DC: U.S. Government Printing Office.

Mech, E. (1988). Preparing foster adolescents for self-support: A new challenge for child welfare services. *Child Welfare, 67,* 487–496.

Mech, E., Pryde, J., & Ryecraft. (1995). Mentors for adolescents in foster care. *Child and Adolescent Social Work Journal, 12,* 317–328.

Mendel, R. (1995). *The American school-to-career movement: A background paper for policymakers and foundation officers.* Washington, DC: American Youth Policy Forum.

Murnane, R.J, Willett, J.B., & Boudett, K.P. (1995). Do high school dropouts benefit from obtaining a GED? *Educational Evaluation and Policy Analysis, 17*(2), 133–147.

New York City Board of Education. (1996). *Assessment/accountability report: The class of 1993.* New York: Author.

North, J., Mallabar, M., & Desrochers, R. (1988). Vocational Preparation and Employability Development. *Child Welfare, 67,* 573–586.

Orfield, G., & Paul, F. (1994). *High hopes, long odds.* Indianapolis: Indiana Youth Institute.

Phillips, L., Votey, H.L., Jr., & Maxwell, D. (1972). Crime, youth, and the labor market. *Journal of Political Economy,* 491–504.

Ricketts, E.R., & Sawhill, I.V. (1988). Defining and measuring the underclass. *Journal of Policy Analysis and Management, 7,* 316–325.

Ringel, C. (1997, November). *Criminal victimization 1996.* Washington, DC: Bureau of Justice Statistics.

Roaf, P.A., Tierney, J.P., & Hunte, D.E. (1994). *Big Brothers/Big Sisters: A study of volunteer recruitment and screening.* Philadelphia: Public/Private Ventures.

Roman, N.P., & Wolfe, P.B. (1997). The relationship between foster care and homelessness. *Public Welfare, 55,* 4–11.

Rumberger, R.W. (1995). Dropping out of middle school: A multi-level analysis of students and schools. *American Educational Research Journal, 32,* 583–625.

Russell, L. (1989). *The GED testing program.* Washington, DC: ERIC Clearinghouse on Tests, Measurement, and Evaluation.

Rylance, B.J. (1997). Predictors of high school graduation or dropping out for youths with severe emotional disturbances. *Behavioral Disorders, 23,* 5–17.

Sampson, R.J. (1997). The embeddedness of child and adolescent development: A comnity-level perspective on urban violence. In J. McCord (Ed.), *Violence and childhood in the inner city,* New York: Cambridge University Press.

Schochet, P.Z., Burghardt, J., & Glazerman, S. (2000, February 9). *National Job Corps study: The short-term impacts of Job Corps on participants' employment and related outcomes.* Final report submitted to the U.S. Department of Labor. Princeton, NJ: Mathematica Policy Research, Inc.

Schorr, L. (1989). *Within our reach: Breaking the cycle of disadvantage.* New York: Anchor Press.

Schwartz, W. (1995). *August 1995 school dropouts: New information about an old problem.* New York: ERIC Clearinghouse on Urban Education.

Smith. S., Blank, S., & Collins, R. (1992). *Pathways to self-sufficiency for two generations.* New York: Foundation for Child Development.

Stern, D. (1997). Learning and earning: The value of working for urban students. *ERIC Digest,* number 128. ERIC Clearinghouse on Urban Education. New York: Columbia University.

Thornberry, I., Moore, M., & Christenson, R. (1985). The effect of dropping out of high school on subsequent criminal behavior. *Criminology, 23,* 3–18.

Tierney, J.P., & Grossman, J. (1995). *Making a difference: An impact study.* Philadelphia: Public/Private Ventures.

United States Census Bureau. (1997). *Educational attainment in the United States, March 1990 and March 1991.* Washington, DC: Author.

United States Department of Education. (1996). *Condition of education.* Washington, DC: National Center for Education Statistics.

United States Department of Labor. (1998). *About youth opportunities.* Washington, DC: Author.

United States Department of Labor. (1999). *Futurework: Trends and challenges for work in the 21st century.* Washington DC: Author.

Vondracek, F.W. (1993). Promoting vocational development in early adolescence. In R.M. Lerner (Ed.), *Early adolescence* (pp. 277–292). Hillsdale, NJ: Lawrence Erlbaum Associates.

Wagner, M.M., & Blackorby, J. (1996). Transition from high school to work or college: How special education students fare. *The Future of Children, 6,* 103–120.

Walker, G. (1997). *Out of school and unemployed: Principles for more effective policy and programs.* Philadelphia: Public/Private Ventures.

West, C. (1993). *Race matters.* Boston: Beacon Press.

Westat. (1989). *A national evaluation of Title IV-E foster care independent living programs for youth.* Final report, phase 1. Rockville, MD: Author.

Westat. (1991). *A national evaluation of Title IV-E foster care independent living programs.* Final report, phase 2. Rockville, MD: Author.

William T. Grant Foundation, Commission on Work, Family and Citizenship. (1988). *The forgotten half: Pathways to success for America's youth and young families (final report).* Washington, DC: Author.

About the Authors

Amy J.L. Baker, Ph.D., is currently the director of research at The Children's Village in Dobbs Ferry, NY. She earned her Ph.D. in developmental psychology from Teachers College of Columbia University. Prior to her directorship at CV, she was director of research at the NCJW Center for the Child, an applied research institute in New York City. Her areas of expertise include early intervention research, parent involvement in the public schools, home visiting programs, and child welfare.

David Olson, Ph.D., is a research associate at The Children's Village. He received his Ph.D. in political science from the State University of New York at Albany. Previously he was director of the Crime Mapping Laboratory at the Police Foundation in Washington, DC. Areas of research interest include youth employment, juvenile delinquency, and urban sociology.

Carolyn Mincer, M.P.H., has been a member of The Children's Village Department of Research and Program Evaluation since 1993. Formerly senior editor on the department's limited-circulation journal, she worked extensively on the final report to the United States Department of Labor, which funded the four-year replication project of the Way program. A graduate of Vassar College, she earned a masters of public health in epidemiology from Columbia University.